53 Questions and Answers about Modules and Semesters

Professor Graham Badley

Head, Anglia Centre for Educational Development

Anglia Polytechnic University

Professor Steve Marshall

Pro Vice Chancellor,

Anglia Polytechnic University

First published in 1995 by
Technical and Educational Services Ltd.
37 Ravenswood Road
Bristol BS6 6BW
UK

ISBN 0 947885 90 0

Printed in Great Britain by The Cromwell Press Ltd., Melksham, Wilts.

Questions and
Answers
about Modules and
Semesters

P. 48.1
9.99
JRJ
(Bad)

0 947885900

Other books by Technical and Educational Services

The '53' series
53 Interesting Things to Do in Your Lectures
53 Interesting Things to Do in Your Seminars and Tutorials
53 Interesting Ways to Assess Your Students
53 Interesting Ways of Helping Your Students to Study
53 Interesting Communication Exercises for Science Students
53 Interesting Ways to Appraise Your Teaching
53 Interesting Ways to Teach Mathematics
53 Interesting Problems with Large Classes: Making the Best of a Bad Job
53 Interesting Ways to Write Open Learning Materials
53 Interesting Activities for Open Learning Courses
53 Interesting Ways to Promote Equal Opportunities in Education

Interesting ways tot each
Preparing to Teach: An Introduction to Effective Teaching in Higher
    Education
253 Ideas for Your Teaching
Interesting Ways to Teach: 12 Do-It-Yourself Staff Development Exer-
    cises
Creating a Teaching Profile

Other titles
Getting the Most from Your Data: Practical Ideas on how to Analyse
    Qualitative Data
Writing Study Guides
Improving the Quality of Student Learning
HMA Stationery Ltd

About the authors

Professor Graham Badley is Head of the Anglia Centre for Educational Development at Anglia Polytechnic University. He is particularly interested in learning about educational improvement through membership of the Staff and Educational Development Association (SEDA) and through a long-standing and continuing study of higher education in the USA.

Professor Steve Marshall is a Pro-Vice-Chancellor at Anglia Polytechnic University with overall responsibility for Human Resources and a coordinating role in one of the teaching faculties. He is particularly interested in the impact of mass higher education on teaching and learning and on the student experience and is keen to ensure that massification brings with it a democratisation of access to higher education.

Acknowledgements

Our wives for letting us spend Sunday afternoons writing.
Our secretaries - Dorothy Boswell, Marga King and Marie McFarlane - for processing the text (and rescuing it when we pressed the wrong buttons).

Sue and Trevor Habeshaw for their help, encouragement and constructive criticism.

Colleagues at Anglia too numerous to mention who argued with us until we thought our ideas were clear.

Contents

Modules

Introduction

Modularity has been around for quite some time. Semesters have existed for even longer. But only comparatively recently have either begun to dominate conversations in staff common rooms.

The reasons for this have a lot to do with the massification of H.E., and the shortage of resources from which we currently suffer. Against this sort of background, academics find themselves under pressure to teach students in larger groups, which could all too easily have the effect of squeezing out of existence the less "popular" subjects.

Modularity, properly implemented, can offer a way forward. By presenting learning in relatively small packages, it makes it possible to use certain modules to contribute to a number of study programmes, offering some prospect of preserving less well-subscribed courses by teaching their students alongside others from areas which find it easier to recruit.

The reason why semesterisation so often comes along with modularity is intimately linked to considerations of teaching and learning. Modularity inevitably leads to some degree of fragmentation of the curriculum, though the better modular schemes usually find effective ways of mitigating the effects of this. Traditional terms tend to accentuate the fragmentation, since they are relatively short. Semesters provide a fairly simple mechanism for breaking down the curriculum into larger units than are likely to occur in term-based systems.

Both modules and semesters imply change from existing and often cherished practices. Change is usually uncomfortable to live with. Occasionally it can provoke real, and sometimes well-founded anxiety. In this little book we attempt to demystify modules and semesters, and to show what kinds of things can be done to ensure that their introduction helps us meet the needs of our students in new ways, while avoiding some of the pitfalls which lurk in wait for the unwary.

The 53 items in this book all consist of questions we have identified as the ones which seem most frequently to concern ourselves, our colleagues and friends, with the answers which seem to us right in terms of our own (fairly extensive) experience of modularity and semesterisation, and what we have learned from talking to others who have grappled with the problems. We have organised the fifty-three items thematically, so that readers can quickly find the issues which concern them, without needing necessarily to plough through the whole text - though we hope many people will!

We have also used the materials in this book to stimulate discussion about modules and semesters during staff development sessions. One way we tried at a recent SEDA conference was to distribute copies of the contents list of questions to a workshop group. Participants were then asked to

• select a question that interests them
• read the answer we provide in the book (the book can be broken up for workshop purposes!)
• get ready to summarise our answer to the group
• comment on our answer
• ask for comments from the group

This actually works. We hope to hear from you if you find other ways of using the material in this book to continue the debate about modules and semesters.

We hope our readers will enjoy reading the book as much as we did writing it, and will come away from it feeling modules and semesters are more friendly than they at first sight may appear, again as happened to us in writing it.

Chapter 1
Technical questions

1 What are modules?
2 Aren't modules American?
3 How can you design modules?
4 What is a module reference sheet?
5 What, in the context of modularity, are learning outcomes?
6 Aren't modules just about credit accumulation and transfer?
7 What are modular levels?
8 Don't modules make degree classifications redundant?

What are modules? 1

Modules are self-contained units which, in an educational context, provide students with specific learning experiences.

In effect a module is a unit or block of learning which, when added to other units, helps to make up a complete course or programme of studies.

Unfortunately the terms *module, unit, course* and *course unit* are often used interchangeably in education, resulting in considerable confusion. Any one university or college will stipulate its own definition which may or may not be acceptable elsewhere.

Generally, however, a module is a measured unit which is part of an extended course of learning leading to the award of a specific qualification. Normally each qualification will require students to complete a set number of designated modules. In a typical UK course scheme for the award of a bachelor's degree students would take 36 modules over three academic years and would, usually, be expected to pass in each module.

However all of this indicates that those designing a modular course scheme have to make decisions about the *size* of each module, the *study pattern* and the *assessment* process as well as such issues as the *value* (or credit-rating) of each module, the *options* or *choices* allowed and the *delivery* (or teaching and learning) systems employed.

* Size
  The size of a module is normally presented as a specified amount of time per week or term or semester or year. Typically a student would be expected to devote, say, 75 hours of study to a particular module in order to achieve its stated learning outcomes. That 75 hours could include, say, 30 hours of class contact time depending on the delivery (teaching/learning) system employed. Most modular systems in UK higher education adopt a standard module size although they would

also allow for double or triple or half modules for various (mainly educational) reasons. The Open University, somewhat unusually, originally designed its modules (which it calls units) to be each one year long and to restrict its students to taking no more than two modules/units per year.

In the USA the term module is rarely used in quite the same way as in the UK; instead, size is determined by the 'credit hour' which represents one hour of contact time per week per term (or quarter) or per semester. Most US modules are, in fact, called courses and are taught for three or four hours per week for a term or for a semester. (See Item 2 below)

- Study pattern
  Modular study patterns vary between the relatively common *concurrent* model where full time students take up to 4 modules per term and the *consecutive* model where students concentrate on one module at a time.

- Assessment
  The assessment process in modular course schemes usually requires that each module is assessed on completion of its taught element. One important consequence of modularity is therefore that each module completed by students is assumed to represent content and outcomes which they have mastered and for which they need never again to be assessed.

Aren't modules American? 2

The term module is not widely-used in the USA to mean a course unit. Where we would use 'module' Americans would mostly use 'course'. We would normally refer to a modular course scheme whereas Americans would more typically refer to a credit system.

However even if modules themselves are not as American as the star-spangled banner they are, nevertheless, an American invention. The idea of modular or elective courses for students was introduced at Harvard by President Eliot in 1869.

By the beginning of the twentieth-century the elective or modular credit system had evolved as a way of loosening the grip of the traditional curriculum and of allowing students to exercise greater freedom in choosing courses (modules) in order to create their own programme.

However, freeing up the curriculum for students soon led to an accompanying need or demand for greater control by the universities themselves. Electives (or modules) had to be quantified in some way so that the new free curriculum could be readily aggregated for the purposes of assessment. Hence the invention of that other great Americanisation - the credit system, a form of curricular accounting or credit banking which is now widespread in North America and is rapidly increasing in the U.K.

However it is worth noting that any modular credit accumulation system in itself will not inevitably lead to greater student autonomy or more curricular coherence. Instead it could lead to greater institutional control over the curriculum and to fragmentation.

Thus modules were and still are American and they bring with them a typical set of American virtues (such as greater freedom?) and American vices (such as more curricular fragmentation?).

How can you design modules? 3

Modules are, in effect, courses or course units. So if we believe that we can design courses then we can quite obviously also design modules.

The trouble is that we in higher education have traditionally been rather poor at course design. So how should we go about the design process? What we need is a design method which fosters a *deep* as opposed to a *surface* approach to learning. Course and module design needs to embody the four key elements of *intrinsic motivation* where students become involved in selecting and planning their own learning, *learning activity* where students are active and reflective rather than passively receptive, *interaction with others* where students negotiate meaning during discussion and a *well-structured knowledge base* where students are helped to make sense of new subject-matter by its being related to their existing knowledge and experience (see Gibbs 1992 for a much fuller discussion of these issues).

More specifically a module may be designed

- by defining a discrete topic or subject area which is small enough and yet coherent enough to be studied within the agreed constraints (and opportunities) of time, staff expertise, material resources, accommodation and student numbers/background

- by considering its possible relationship with other modules in order to avoid unnecessary overlap or duplication and to complement their content and intended outcomes

- by carefully stating its expected learning outcomes in terms of what students should be able to do as a result of completing the module

- by basing assessment practices on the intended learning outcomes

- by choosing module content and its teaching/learning processes following analysis of the intended outcomes and their assessment.

The important issue here is that modules can be designed to encourage meaningful learning if designers move away from a traditional over-concern with subject content and towards a greater emphasis on process, especially through the use of strategies which encourage more student involvement and learner activity. The danger with a modular scheme is that modules will be packed with more and more content and that students will be forced into a rather superficial view of their learning tasks.

What is a module reference sheet?   4

Some universities now encourage staff to design their modules in such a way that they can be displayed simply on a 'module reference sheet' which may contain the following information:

1 Module title   e.g.   Action Research and Social Inquiry
2 Credits and level   30 at Level M
3 Set   e.g.   Post-compulsory education
4 Keywords   Action Research, Social Inquiry
5 Prerequisites and corequisites   None
6 Learning outcomes (usually expressed in terms of what the student will be able to do) e.g.
   i   Draw upon a range of theory to address problems in social inquiry
   ii   Make a personal interpretation of theory for inquiring into social issues
   iii   Create an evaluative synthesis in the form of a commentary on an action research project
7 Catalogue summary
8 Delivery method
9 Indicative learning activities
10 Indicative assessment
11 Indicative assessment schedule
12 Indicative outline content
13 Indicative learning resources / support
   (especially key texts and other media).

There is sufficient opportunity here (in about two A4 pages) for the module designer to indicate how a deep approach to learning will be encouraged. The module's learning outcomes, learning activities, assessment and content should indicate the extent to which the design has sought to feature such typical educational strategies as independent learning, problem-based learning, reflection, group work, learning by doing and project work (see Gibbs 1992 for a useful account of these strategies).

What, in the context of modularity, 5 are learning outcomes?

Learning outcomes are not much different from behavioural objectives, which forced many a teacher, particularly in further education colleges, to write more and more precise statements of what their students should be able to do as a result of their teaching.

Objectives should preferably be written using clear terms which describe only the specific observable behaviour intended. In order to reduce ambiguity writers of objectives are expected to state the *terminal behaviour* to be demonstrated by the student at the end of the course, the main *conditions* under which the terminal behaviour would occur and the *criteria* to be used to judge acceptable performance. Such an approach would reject objectives expressed using action verbs like 'know', 'understand' and 'appreciate' because of their vagueness and their inability to describe precise terminal behaviour. Objectives, instead, should be expressed by using verbs such as 'state' or 'write' or 'list' or 'select' which could more precisely specify observable behaviour. The conditions referred to could include the fact that for example students could or could not use reference books or equipment (such as calculators) to demonstrate achievement of objectives. *Criteria* would be specified to indicate the standard or quality or extent of attainment.

In higher education, however, specifying behavioural objectives has mainly been resisted for a large number of reasons which include

- the difficulty and/or undesirability of specifying behaviour in certain subjects (especially in the arts)

- the problem of detail - how specific should objectives be?

- the problem of time - specifying all possible objectives for a course or module would consume too much time

- the danger of triviality - the easiest behaviours to specify are the most trivial

- the danger of restriction - by specifying objectives the excitement of discovery learning could be missed

- the danger of dogmatism - that these are the right objectives for this subject

- the danger of limiting teaching-student interaction - to the mere achievement of behavioural objectives.

On the other hand many staff in higher education appreciate the opportunity of using objectives in a less strict or formal way because it enables them to be clearer in their curriculum planning, to communicate course intentions more effectively to students, to select appropriate course content, teaching and learning methods and to guide them in the choice of assessment methods.

Consequently staff in higher education have adopted, in general, a less strict and less formal view of expressing course objectives than was the case in much of further education.

They have tended not to over-elaborate their specification of course or module objectives and have rarely adopted the National Vocational Qualification (NVQ) model of placing them in hierarchical order.

For the most part, therefore, module designers tend to use the idea of learning outcomes rather than strict behavioural objectives and have tended to adopt a rather pragmatic approach to their specification. They would horrify strict behaviourists since they often do use words like 'understand', 'know' and 'appreciate' on the basis that they, as tutors, are capable of showing students what it means to understand or know a subject or appreciate the strengths of an argument and to indicate to students how they can demonstrate their understanding, knowing or appreciating as part of the assessment process. The confusion over the use of the terms 'learning outcomes' and 'learning objectives' is probably because staff in higher education use both terms pragmatically and rather vaguely. In such modular schemes there is, interestingly enough, no definition of learning outcomes. Instead many in higher education have adopted a way of expressing learning outcomes or general learning objectives as statements of what students should be able to do when learning has been achieved successfully. Indeed, HEFCE guidelines require that course descriptions will include statements of aims and learning outcomes (HEFCE circular 39/94).

Aren't modules just about credit accumulation and transfer?   6

Much of what we have said in this book in answer to the other questions posed attests to the fact that modules and modularisation are and could be about many things. Depending on how we set about the task of designing and delivering modules they can help us to encourage and enhance student motivation, active, deep learning, group interaction and the acquisition of structured knowledge. We can so choose modular learning outcomes that they will enable students to develop both specific competencies and general transferable skills as well as promote the advancement of learning and culture. We can emphasise modular assessment strategies which demonstrate that modular learning is about meaning and understanding and not about memory and regurgitation. And modules are also a way for students to earn credit for their work and achievements.

It is true, of course, that modularisation and credit transfer have become the academic currency of the marketplace especially in the USA.

It is this desire for greater flexibility, mobility and transfer which has stimulated the creation of, first, the Educational Counselling and Credit Transfer Information Service (ECCTIS) and then the CNAA's Credit Accumulation and Transfer Scheme (CATS).

CAT schemes have now expanded to become institutional policy first among the former polytechnics and, more recently, among universities. In this sense a national framework is emerging through consensus and practice among higher education institutions.

Credit accumulation and transfer is happening : because most colleges and universities now want to extend *access* to those with non-traditional qualifications; because many are trying not to exclude those who cannot or do not wish to study full-time; because some wish to allow those whose circumstances change to adjust their programmes of study; because some want to allow those who couldn't, because of poverty or other circumstances, start higher education at 18 to have a further chance; because several want to help students to integrate prior learning gained outside higher education with that learning gained inside higher education; and many colleges and universities want to provide opportunities for continuing education generally (see Davidson 1992, p177).

Not all of this is, of course, strictly altruistic. Many colleges and universities do have mission statements which stress the extension of opportunities for higher education to all who can benefit (a very Robbins-like ambition) and particularly to those under-represented groups such as ethnic minorities, the disadvantaged and the disabled by using appropriately responsive patterns of teaching and learning to enable smooth progression and flexible higher education opportunity. Colleges and universities claim that their flexible modular and credit-based curriculum will provide a basis for the further development of responsive and accessible opportunities across the region. But, of course, they also think that their CAT scheme will enable them to recruit more students (and keep them in business) and especially those to whom they have offered access opportunities by providing franchised courses in local further education and sixth-form colleges.

Modularity is not however just about credit accumulation and transfer. It can aid the extension of access and the recognition of learning across the traditional boundaries between universities and other institutions. It can help students accumulate their awards according to their own circumstances. Modularity can facilitate credit accumulation and transfer. But we think it ought to be more about the promotion of lifelong learning than about the accumulation of academic credit, valuable though that is.

What are modular levels?   7

Modules may be delivered and assessed at a number of levels which are thought to indicate differences in standard.   Typically most modular schemes in higher education are assessed at four levels which correspond to First Year, Second Year, Third Year and Post Graduate studies.

One not untypical scheme also has four levels, defined as follows:

Level A: Degree entry, Access study

Level B: Basic study: assessed at first year full-time degree standard

Level H: Higher study: assessed at honours degree standard

Level M: Advanced study assessed at Masters degree level, assuming honours degree competences.

These statements about modular levels apparently show a considerable amount of confidence in an ability to distinguish one level from another. Unfortunately, however, regulations often fail to specify what is meant by Level A and appear to make the assumption, justified or not, that this level is so well-known that it doesn't require definition.   Some schemes do attempt to specify a range of assessment criteria with terms such as 'a clear understanding of the assessment task', 'to be articulate' in expressing ideas in mainly 'descriptive' or 'imitative' ways, 'understanding of the theoretical background' and ' analytic competence'.

Level H criteria typically specify 'the individual's increasing autonomy', 'ability in problem solving skills', 'understanding of appropriate theory', 'creativity of expression and thought' and 'the ability to seek out, invoke, analyse and evaluate competing theories'. The main differences between Level B (Basic) and Level H (Higher) would appear to be a move towards greater student autonomy and creativity although there is an implication that students should also be assessed according to more developed abilities to understand , analyse and evaluate theory.

At Level M (Masters) students should presumably be assessed on their subject 'expertise', their 'independence in negotiation of assessment tasks' and 'the ability to evaluate, challenge, modify and develop theory and practice'. Students, at this level, should also be expected 'to offer synthetic and coherent solutions' and to show 'potential for leading others in the specialist area'.

However it has been pointed out that many of the terms that educationalists use to characterise different educational stages or levels, and especially those used to offer criteria for assessment from GCE A level through to Master's level, are so remarkably similar that they may *not* be invoked to clarify differences between one higher education stage and another.

Winter, having analysed a variety of data derived mainly from tutors' comments on students' work in higher education, showed that the *distinctive* features of higher education are not analysis, synthesis or critical evaluation as such but "those which demonstrate a capacity for relatively *autonomous* learning, and those which demonstrate a *personal* synthesis derived from both *practical experience* and from *reading*" . At postgraduate level the same assessment vocabulary is employed as at A level and undergraduate levels with two exceptions: *students' commitment to a specialism* and *the external value of students' work* (see Winter 1994, pp8-9).

Following this analysis we can conclude that defining modular levels is a far from simple process given that the assessment criteria we tend to use are continuous from A level to postgraduates level. The criteria we use to distinguish level B from level H and level M are, in fact, either explicit or implicit at all levels.

One solution to the problem of distinguishing modular levels may be summarised as follows:

1   Learning outcomes must include general learning abilities in order to make explicit 'the full extent of the learning process' in each module;

2   Level-(or stage-) related criteria must be fulfilled in some but not all modules; at the undergraduate level learning outcomes should include autonomous forms of learning, at the postgraduate level outcomes should indicate specialist commitment and scholarship; but these are demands for each award as a whole and they need not be required of each module;

3   Each award must include an integrative unit which requires of students their rationale for the selection of various modules and which shows how the understanding derived from one module supports the learning required by others;

4   Modules may identify prerequisites and corequisites in order to allow change and variability (based on Winter 1994, pp10-12).

This proposal is an attempt to allow for student or learner progression towards *increasing personal autonomy and commitment* by focusing on the educational *aims or outcomes* of each modular level rather than on the levels themselves as hierarchical or managerial categories which is what they may, in fact, become. Again, therefore, it's up to us. Modular levels can be about educational aims or about hierarchies.

Don't modules make degree classifications redundant?   8

Since modules are self-contained units of study, separately assessed, it is normal for students to receive feedback, in the form of assessment results, throughout a modular course. Although in many cases it is specifically stated that the marks issued are subject to moderation by external assessors, nonetheless by the end of a programme of study, students have a good idea, and sometimes a fairly precise knowledge, of the class of degree they can expect.

It is also the case that many, and possibly most, modular courses issue a transcript at the end of the course showing the precise result achieved in each module.

It is in the light of these facts that many argue that the traditional classification of Honours Degrees is made redundant by modularity. The arguments are both pragmatic and academic.

The pragmatic argument is that, in an age when litigation is an ever more present factor in all aspects of life, and rapidly increasing in HE, it is extremely risky to award a class of honours on any basis other than straight aggregation of marks, given that students will know the marks and could challenge in court any variation from the award they seem to have earned through their marks. If this is the case, why bother to classify, rather than simply issuing a detailed transcript, or a Grade Point Average?

The academic argument is that classification has always been a blunt instrument. Academics spend many hours agonising over the process of attaching a precise mark to a piece of work. At the end of the process each assessed item has a mark of, for example, 62, 53, A++-, B+(?)-, etc. Then, having achieved a high level of precision, we abandon the whole thing and attach to students a label which, in itself, does not distinguish between a mark of 59 and one of 50. Is it not better, it is argued, to give more precise guidance to graduates and their prospective employers by issuing a detailed transcript, or a Grade Point Average?

Against these arguments it is protested that strictly numerical systems remove all discretion from assessors, who are therefore unable to take steps to recognise exceptional quality of mind where it is displayed in part, but not all, of the assessments undergone. To which the supporters of transcripts retort that if assessment is properly conducted, and both internal and external assessors are confident that marks are accurate, it is absurd to then abandon the systematic approach and instead substitute personal judgement to second guess the right result.

The argument seems set to rage for some time before being resolved. For the moment, opponents of classification are probably still in a minority. We believe, however, that eventually classification will be seen to be appropriate only in the context of traditional courses structures, and will be abandoned by modular institutions.

Chapter 2

Policy questions

9   Aren't modules too small for higher education purposes?

10   How should module delivery be seen in the context of the university as a whole?

11   Are modular courses really as flexible as some proponents claim?

12   Are modules more about cost-effectiveness and efficiency than learning?

13   Are modules more about marketing than education?

14   Modularisation is a solution - what's the problem?

15   Modularisation is just rhetoric - isn't it old wine in new bottles?

16   Doesn't modularisation produce a *smörgasbord* approach to higher education?

17   Isn't it true that modularisation doesn't really happen in the best universities?

18   Wasn't modularisation actually forced on the universities?

19   Aren't modules actually about improving general education, and isn't higher education actually about specialisation?

20   Can modular systems cope with the demands of professional courses?

Aren't modules too small for higher education purposes?   9

What purposes does higher education actually have? According to the Robbins' Report of 1963, the last great official statement on Higher Education in the UK, we have to acknowledge a plurality of purposes or general social ends which should be served by higher education. These purposes, crudely summarised, are:

- instruction in skills
- promotion of the general powers of the mind
- the advancement of learning
- the transmission of a common culture and common standards of citizenship

(see Robbins (1963) pp6-7).

Obviously Robbins was reporting on the higher education system as a whole. But we think that these same purposes could be served to some extent by individual modules.

i **Instruction in skills**
   Thus we could ask whether a 30 hour taught module could possibly help in the development of important skills. Obviously any one module can only have a limited number of learning outcomes but it seems to us that even with such a small module (typically taught for 3 hours per week for 10 weeks) a number of important skills can be taught and learnt. For example students can be taught, as part of such a module, communication and teamwork skills which we are continuously being told are essential in the contemporary world of work.

ii **Promotion of the general powers of the mind**
What Robbins vaguely called 'the general powers of the mind' requires that these practical skills are taught in such a way that they are applicable to many problems, that they are taught in the more current phrase as transferable skills. Surely our modules no matter how small they appear to be can offer to meet such a broad educational purpose?

iii **The advancement of learning**
Not all modules (and probably not those at first or second year levels) will promote the advancement of learning. They would not be expected to. However those modules in the final year or at postgraduate level which encourage and/or require problem-solving, independent learning, reflection and project work are essentially focused on discovery and as such contribute, often no doubt in a small way, to the advancement of learning in general.

iv **The transmission of a common culture and common standards of citizenship**
Robbins admitted that it was difficult to describe the transmission of culture and citizenship concisely. Nevertheless higher educational institutes should, he maintained, create an atmosphere conducive to work and cultural life especially in the provision of equal opportunities. Even relatively small modules can contribute to some extent to the development of an appropriate cultural and civic ethos.

However, we could see a better contribution to all these main purposes of higher education if our modules were, say, at least a semester long rather than delivered within the shorter confines of a term. Having said that we also recognise that the notion of purpose in higher education is a highly contested question which we have only touched upon in this section.

And again if our main purpose is to cram as much content into our modules as possible without having any real regard for meeting other educational purposes then, of course, modules are too small. Modules are, in effect, containers : and we can't put a quart in a pint pot.

Also the smaller the module the more likely it is that staff (and students) will complain of lack of depth and superficiality. Some will argue that a modular approach will necessarily fragment subject-matter and prevent a holistic approach to learning. Small modules, even those delivered in 10 weeks, will also almost inevitably lead to over-assessment (see item 26) unless a way can be found to assess different modules together.

How should module delivery be seen 10 in the context of the university as a whole?

Staff don't just design and deliver modules independently, although there was a time, in the not too distant past, when course design and evaluation were, indeed, fairly autonomous and unregulated academic pursuits. Requiring staff to be more explicit about their course aims and objectives, their course content, their preferred teaching and learning methods and their assessment practices owes much to the pioneering work of the Open University and to the Council for National Academic Awards.

Module and course design and delivery are now clearly recognised as two main events in a relatively complicated series of transactions which impact on staff, institutional resources, student services, the students themselves and, as the Robbins Report also emphasised, society itself. These transactions can be presented more simply in a model which we have adapted from Mantz Yorke's paper on Quality in Higher Education (1992).

The main focus of attention in the model (overleaf) is on students who are characterised more and more as 'informed consumers exercising choice'. Courses, and the modules which make them up, therefore have to satisfy their consumers' expectations, including their desire for learning outcomes which do meet their own and society's needs for the various transferable skills and structured knowledge now deemed desirable and relevant. As Yorke points out students *and* society are *both* customers of the modules and courses delivered by our higher education institutions.

However one problem with the notion of modular or course *delivery* is that students may be visualised simply as customers who pay for a product which is deposited, like the morning milk, on their doorsteps. Course and module delivery, particularly of the kind we've emphasised which stresses

Some transactions associated with module and course delivery. *After Yorke (1992)*

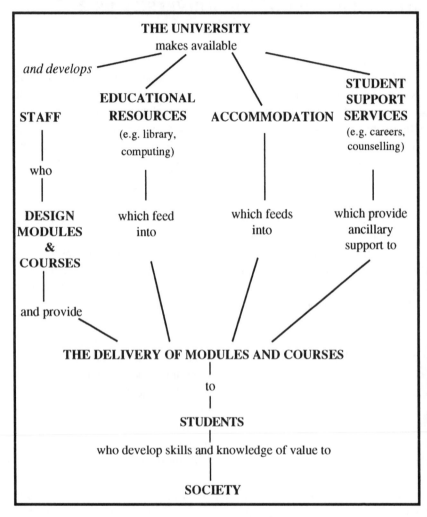

meaning and understanding, is not about transmission but more about transformation. Ideas, concepts, principles and subject content are not just packaged into convenient containers to be dumped on students for storage and, at some stage, for use if one can be found. The kind of delivery we espouse is one which stimulates students to become engaged as active participants in the learning process so that their understanding of key ideas, concepts and subject-matter transforms them from learners into knowers.

Yorke's model does, however, permit us to envisage module and course delivery in these participative and transforming ways just so long as we build into the system of transactions the notion that delivery is not *to* or *for* students but *with* and *by* students.

Perhaps we need to imagine module 'delivery' more in terms of the midwife enabling and supporting childbirth - the midwife doesn't deliver, the mother does. So the university or the staff or the course or the module don't deliver the learning outcomes to the students as such : instead the students are supported and empowered by the university, the staff, the resources provided, the accommodation used, the student services employed, the course and the modules undertaken to deliver their own learning for assessment.

Are modular courses really as 11
flexible as some proponents claim?

The American credit hour or modular system supposedly provides the most flexible higher education programmes in the world. Students gain their degrees through the accumulation of 40 (semester) to 60 (term) courses (or modules worth three credit hours) over a four-year period. Thus each year students would usually take 10 or 15 courses, either five per semester or five per term. Obviously the term -based courses taught for 10 weeks at three contact hours per week, represent smaller modules than the semester-based courses, 15 weeks at three hours per week.

Either way the accumulation of courses or modules is supposed to offer students considerable flexibility and choice. However, a modular course without choice and flexibility is quite possible given that modular scheme leaders have several ways of imposing restrictions on students. Students may be *required* to take particular modules for a particular qualification or to select a fixed number of modules from a set. Students may also be *restricted* from choosing certain numbers or types of modules. Many modular schemes have *prerequisites* which limit entry to modules to those students who have met the learning outcomes of a specified module or modules. Modules are also often provided at different *levels* (for example at level 3 or third year) which may then restrict entry to students in a particular year of study. Groups of modules may also be offered as *sets, streams, strands, pathways, series, fields or corequisites* so that students may be expected to keep within a chosen route through the modular maze. Some students may need *special permission* to undertake specific modules or may be *excluded* from modules because they are deemed to lack prior knowledge or skills or because the module is regarded as inappropriate to their chosen programme of study. Also modules become *unavailable* for a variety of reasons including timetabling difficulties and previous unpopularity (with students) or perceived difficulty (for staff and/or students). A modular system employing all of the above devices may in practice be highly restrictive.

Thus if we want a modular system to be flexible, and most of us claim that we do, we shall resist the temptation to pack our particular scheme full of those requirements, restrictions, prerequisites, corequisites and other exclusions which would render the scheme more rigid than a traditional university single honours course. On the other hand the persistent and clamorous demands for quality, for maintaining or even improving standards, for coherence and for progression will tend to make our modular scheme more conservative and even more traditional and less flexible than we (and our students?) would want.

Are modules more about cost-effectiveness and efficiency than learning?   12

If they are then they shouldn't be. Philosophically we don't object to the notion that our universities and colleges should be run efficiently and effectively. Indeed in order to meet the kinds of learning outcomes we are interested in we believe that higher education should be run efficiently and should be cost-effective. The main issue is, however, whether we can be effective in meeting our goals and efficient in meeting them by using our resources appropriately without losing sight of our educational values. We in higher education need a clear sense of mission or purpose which allows us to be both businesslike and true to our educational values.

We don't believe that a modular programme, which we think *could be* a relatively effective, efficient and businesslike way of delivering the curriculum to large numbers of students in a mass higher education system, are necessarily antithetical or alien to a typical range of educational and intellectual values such as knowledge, understanding, truth, beauty, mutual respect, freedom, intellectual discipline, criticism, communication, breadth, depth, coherence and progression. Indeed many of the modules already validated and taught embody some of these values.

There is a danger of course that if modules are seen only as ways of banking credit then their educational value in providing interesting learning experiences for students will be discounted. Again the point is that we can make modularity do for us almost whatever we want. We could become more apparently efficient by concentrating on the delivery of popular modules to large numbers of students. Or we could attempt to meet broader educational goals by adopting a much more balanced approach. It's up to us.

47

Are modules more about marketing than education? 13

For the past 15 years higher education institutions have been continuously urged to become more market-oriented and more entrepreneurial. What this has often meant is that universities and colleges were expected by their funding bodies, and ultimately by H.M. Government acting on behalf of the taxpayer, to become more consumer- or client-centred and less provider-centred. Academics were expected to descend occasionally from their ivory (or breeze-block) towers and see what was happening in the real world of business and industry, where the resources which they used up were actually created.

In the 1980's particularly the former polytechnics adopted a much more market-led approach to their activities. For the first time they wrote strategic plans, mission statements and various business and development plans. Amongst all this came the marketing strategy and, in many instances, the appointment of a Director of Marketing. And, throughout the former polytechnic sector, they also created modular systems.

Is modularity, therefore, mainly about marketing? Modularity and marketing do appear to have much in common. They both appeal to a client or a consumer, they both deal with the creation and delivery of packaged products and services, and they both offer to provide for the needs and wishes of individuals at supposedly convenient times and places. Indeed marketing and modularity both claim not to *sell* products and services as such but rather to *customise* their offerings to suit each particular commission.

Furthermore marketing and modularity are systemic functions. They both claim to adopt a market research approach to discover their clients' needs and wants, they develop specific products or modules to meet those needs, they promote their products and modules through advertising campaigns and glossy brochures, they submit to quality control and quality assurance procedures and they modify and change their products and modules as a result of client feedback and customer satisfaction (or lack of it).

However we believe that modularity need not be thought of as being more about marketing than education. We think that higher education institutions quite rightly should adopt many of the useful and practical aspects of marketing. But educational practice also has its strengths which are often overlooked in a totally market-orientated view of modularity. Some of those strengths also predate the marketing revolution. First, the notion of client-centredness is not too far removed from that of *student-centredness* which has, at least since Rousseau, figured prominently in many an educational establishment. Engaging students in the construction of their own educational programmes has a long and honoured history. Second, the idea of collecting *feedback* on *customer satisfaction* has long since been a feature of good course evaluation procedures particularly in the former polytechnics. Admittedly, however, we haven't been as systematic and as thorough in our collection of feedback data as most American universities. Fortunately both the Higher Education Funding Councils and the Higher Education Quality Council are now expecting much more from higher education institutions in the way of collecting data from student feedback. However the most important strength, from our point of view, is the increasing understanding and use of a sophisticated array of *evaluation and review* procedures which again predate and out-reach the concerns of the market research movement. A useful module was produced by O'Neill and Pennington in 1992 which provided a number of developmental reasons for evaluation, outlined numerous techniques for collecting evidence from students, from teachers themselves and from their peers, presented the portfolio as a way of synthesising evidence and evaluation, and identified ways in which courses (and modules) may be evaluated and reviewed.

We think it is useful to adopt a marketing perspective based on customer needs and satisfactions. But 'customer' and 'client' are only ways of seeing who we are dealing with in the modular systems. The term 'student' is also an honourable and resonant one - we forget it at our peril.

Modularisation is a solution - what's the problem? 14

The garbage can model of educational management claims that educational decision-making is essentially ambiguous. Various problems and solutions are, as it were, thrown into a garbage can by an institution's members. This mix of garbage - problems and solutions - obviously varies at any one time. Decisions are outcomes of the interactions of the various *problems* which have arisen, of the various *solutions* (or answers) which individuals or groups have dumped into the can, the *participants* (who usually identify the problems and contribute the solutions) at the time and the *choice opportunities* when a decision is called for.

In this model modularisation is obviously a solution or an answer which some individuals or groups have regularly and, now, successfully put forward. Modularisation was obviously an original solution to the problem of providing more student-centred learning in Harvard in 1869. The elective system was a solution to the American problem of providing a wide array of curricular choice. The credit system was a solution to the American problem of how various educational experiences could be added up or aggregated or quantified.

What problem or problems does modularisation solve in the UK? The first modular scheme at the University of London in the 1960's was initially an attempt to solve the problem of students registered for special degrees who were unable to get honours in particular subjects. The modular (or course unit) scheme sought a flexible solution to allow a range of options which would provide a broad training for science graduates who might seek non-scientific careers. It was also a solution which was politically acceptable to individual schools of the university since it gave them considerable autonomy including power and control over the combination of courses that their students might take and over the assessment process. The London course unit or modular system did not, apparently, produce solutions to other important problems such as the production of innovatory courses or the development of introductory courses or reducing costs or increasing interschool sharing.

The problem to which the first modular degree at The City of London Polytechnic was a solution in 1973 was the need for greater recruitment and wider access. Recruitment was particularly needed for its science courses which were, in effect, balanced by good recruitment in social science and business courses.

The City modular degree also, in 1979/80, introduced 'majoring' as a solution to the problem of making this rather broad interdisciplinary degree recognised for specialist study.

Oxford Polytechnic's modular course, which in 1972 was the first multi-disciplinary science course validated by the CNAA, seems to have been an attempted solution to various problems including the need for greater curricular choice, for economies of scale and for the introduction of slot timetabling.

Other modular courses have been adopted for a number of explicit reasons including: a long standing commitment to student centred learning, the need to enable students to access learning opportunities in numerous ways, the desire to offer learning opportunities to a wider group of students easily, flexibly and without loss of quality and to recognise that learning occurs in many situations which should be available for credit, provided it can be assessed.

Thus, as these examples demonstrate, modularisation is often thought to be a solution to quite a range of perceived educational problems: to provide more student-centred learning, to provide greater curricular choice, to find a way of crediting or quantifying the educational experience, to provide greater flexibility and breadth, to attract better recruitment and wider access, and, increasingly, to provide economies of scale. Whether any of these problems are actually solved by modularisation is altogether another matter.

And, finally, it is interesting to note that the Labour Party in a recent paper also sees the full modularisation of further and higher education as a solution to a range of social and educational problems: to offer students broader and more flexible opportunities, to help move towards a full-blown national credit accumulation and transfer system, to end the divide between academic and vocational qualifications, to support an expansion of higher education, to broaden A levels whilst maintaining standards, to provide a more coherent 14-19+ curriculum and to create a broader degree structure as a better preparation for careers. Modularisation is *some* solution.

Modularisation is just rhetoric - isn't it   15
old wine in new bottles?

We don't think modularisation is *just* rhetoric but we do agree that it developed with many a rhetorical flourish.

The module in British post-compulsory education has taken on the quality of 'a perpetual novelty' in contrast to what is often perceived in the surrounding curriculum context in which there is too much evidence of 'the dull, the uninspiring, the out-of-date and the irrelevant'. Modularity appears to meet higher education's recurrent need for change and transformation and for showing our paymasters that we are really dynamic, exciting, up-to-date and relevant to every possible social and economic need (so give us the money).

The Labour Party has now put a political twist on modularity which will, it thinks, transform the moribund UK into a dynamic Learning Society for the twenty-first century. It is interesting to note, in this context, that the recent 'Learning Society Programme' (ESRC 1994) asked "Does modularisation impose a strait jacket which inhibits coherence and progress in learning?", a question which seems to carry with it all the old prejudices against any move away from the traditional Honours degree. There's plenty of rhetoric about if we want to listen to it.

Part of the trouble is, of course, that modularity *is* putting old wine in new bottles if that is how we choose to interpret the modular process. Modules are, quite simply, containers - bottles - into which we can just pour the old liquid from our bulk storage tanks. We might, however, choose differently. We might be prepared to be innovative, to design new modules with relevant learning outcomes, interesting content and interactive assessment tasks. As we have already seen it's all up to us.

We must remember, however, that in many senses all teaching and learning in higher education, whether divided into discreet modules or not, is rhetorical. Learning in higher education is not, for the most part, direct learning about the world but rather learning about ways of looking at the world. Higher education is, at the undergraduate level certainly, a mainly second-order activity of reflecting on experience which is mediated by teaching, most of which provides its own descriptions of the world. In this sense 'Teaching is essentially a rhetorical activity, seeking to persuade students to change the way they experience the world. It has to create the environment that will enable students to learn the descriptions of the world devised by others' (Laurillard 1993, p28).

This is not to say that modular learning is inferior to, say, the direct experience of the world which characterises the learning of the research scientist. It is simply to recognise that much of what is done, certainly at the undergraduate level, is learning through description and not learning by direct experience. Of course we can design and deliver some modules in order to provide students with actual or simulated experiences - the most obvious ones are those which provide work experience or immersion in foreign languages - but the great majority of modular learning at the undergraduate level will be rhetorical in the sense that students will learn about the world through, mainly, linguistic descriptions of it constructed by others. Modules need to address, as far as possible, both the direct experience of the world as well as those historical, geographical, literary, scientific and philosophical accounts of it which are the academic's stock-in-trade. Modular learning in this sense is mainly rhetoric, but it is rhetoric seen positively as a way in which students can be helped to become more autonomous and scholarly users of language (and other symbolic systems) as they progressively learn how to criticise and then own their own descriptions of the historical, geographical, literary, scientific and philosophical worlds that they and we inhabit.

Doesn't modularisation produce a smörgasbord approach to higher education? 16

The assumption behind this question is that modularisation isn't a proper way to deliver the curriculum in higher education just as a smörgasbord is assumed to be an inadequate substitute for a proper meal.

There seems to be a certain amount of prejudice at work here. Modularisation, like the smörgasbord, was not invented here, and is therefore automatically suspect.

Secondly, modularisation, like the smörgasbord, appears to be about variety rather than coherence, progression and specialisation. Proper courses in higher education are meant to cohere around a major subject and to progress via a series of levels towards greater mastery over a specialist subject. Modularisation, on the other hand, is thought to offer, like the smörgasbord, tempting morsels which might look attractive but are not fulfilling.

Thirdly, modularisation appears, like the smörgasbord, to be about choice, choice made by the consumer rather imposed by the producer. Those of us who want greater control over the programmes which our students may select will tend to sneer at the chaotic choice offered by modularisation. Instead we may want to deliver the set meal featuring the traditional roast meat and vegetables. By contrast those who offer modularity seem to be offering a wider range of courses, like the smörgasbord, which don't necessarily follow the same structure as more traditional fare.

As always in these conflicts proponents take up entrenched positions. It's either traditional courses or modularity, set meals or the smörgasbord. We like the smörgasbord approach especially where it can be planned to include substantial courses or groups of modules which satisfy students' demands for a certain amount of specialisation within a first degree programme.

We endorse, therefore, the findings of HMI following their study of education in the USA (HMI 1991) when they point out that because of the wide choice and curricular breadth of higher education in the USA (the smörgasbord approach) and the inevitable diversity of learning undertaken by students "there is growing interest in the case of core curricula to ensure that all students are given an opportunity to develop general skills" (HMI 1991, p16). They summarised the core curriculum for undergraduates at the University of Denver which occupies 40-50% of their time and aims to develop:

- a foundation for later studies
- the ability to communicate effectively in written and oral forms
- the capacity for abstract reasoning
- problem solving skills
- an understanding of the physical and social environment
- an appreciation of and respect for the arts
- the ability to use more than one language
- a multicultural and multinational perspective
- a knowledge of the world's great literature
- quantitative skills
- an understanding of the professions and their place in society

(HMI 1991, p16,17).

To dyed-in-the-wool traditionalists this core curriculum still represents a dilution of the specialist nature of the British first degree. Alternatively we think that such an approach, embodied in a range of well-designed modules at appropriate levels, will enable students to meet the general and specific purposes of higher education (see 9 above). If this is characterised as a smörgasbord approach, then so be it.

But what we don't want to happen in the UK is the trivialisation of higher education which a modular approach, improperly managed, has sometimes produced in the USA:

'Much too frequently, American higher education now offers a smörgasbord of fanciful courses in a fragmented curriculum that accords as much credit for "Introduction to Tennis' and for courses in pop culture as it does for 'Principles of English Composition', history, or physics, thereby trivialising education - indeed misleading students by implying that they are receiving the education they need for life when they are not' (Wingspread 1993, p5). It couldn't possibly happen like this here, could it?

Isn't it true that modularisation doesn't really happen in the best universities?   17

Modularisation, in effect, started at Harvard in 1869. Harvard is certainly one of the best universities in the USA and in the world judged by any number of criteria including those relating to quality of research and to quality of teaching.

Modularisation also began in the UK at the University of London in the mid-1960's. The University of London is certainly one of the UK's best universities.

The Open University has offered all its courses on a modular basis since it began teaching its first 25,000 students in January 1971. The Open University has developed into one of the most innovative and successful modern universities in the world.

Numerous other universities including many of the former polytechnics have now established a modular scheme. These include on the one hand former polytechnics such as Oxford Brookes and London Guildhall as well as some 22 of the traditional universities including Stirling, Aberdeen, LSE, King's, Imperial, Newcastle, Liverpool and Brunel; nine other universities have begun to modularise e.g. Bradford, UEA, Exeter, Leeds and Ulster, and that a further nine have agreed in principle to modularise including Birmingham, Bristol, Sheffield and Swansea. Only 5 universities in Davidson's 1992 study (Aston, City, Essex, York and Edinburgh) appeared to show little or no interest in establishing a modular scheme.

Modularisation hasn't of course happened at Oxford or Cambridge. Or has it? There are those who would argue that the Cambridge Tripos has many of the essential features of modularity. Students choose the requisite number of courses from a menu, which enables them to tailor the programme, to some extent, to reflect their own interests. They can often include broadening elements, within limits. And they do this with advice from their Director of Studies. Maybe modularity is really just the rest of the world catching up.

Wasn't modularisation actually forced on the universities?   18

Were they pushed or did they jump? What we appear to be dealing with here is change, change towards modularisation which is the result of a number of strategies some of which appear to be power-coercive (the push) and some of which appear to be normative - re-educative (the jump).

The early adoption of modularisation by the University of London was mainly for internal political reasons. The Science Faculty were not pushed; they saw modularity (their course unit system) as a way of creating individual teacher and school autonomy, giving them freedom from central university control over their courses.

Nor was the Open University pushed into modularity. It decided itself that in order to serve its mature, non-traditional students, a non-traditional modular degree with a strong general educational component (typical of most American undergraduate programmes) was both necessary and desirable.

We have also seen that former polytechnics such as City of London and Oxford Brookes adopted modularity for their own specific purposes - to increase access and recruitment and to provide greater choice as well as economies of scale. Neither university would regard itself as being pushed or coerced into modularity.

Undoubtedly, however, since the 1970's there has been a certain amount of push about. *International pressure* to increase the participation rate in higher education and to move the UK from an elite system to a mass and then to a universal system could be facilitated by the adoption of American-style modularisation with its greater flexibility, access and mobility. As Martin Trow pointed out 'American higher education differs from all others in offering access to some part of the system to almost everyone who wants to go to college or university, without having to show evidence of academic talent or qualification. Private attitudes and public policy .... affirm that the more people who can be persuaded to enrol in a college or university, the better' (Trow 1989).

The UK has gradually come to understand the value of the modular course earning unit-credits, an academic currency that makes a system in the USA out of 3500 separate institutions. And we have also learned, from the USA, that credits that can be accumulated and transferred also allow students to drop out, or stop out, and return to college in ways that are increasingly familiar to us.

Interest in modularisation grew in the UK, particularly in the former polytechnics, during the 1970's so that by 1980 25 out of 29 had at least one modular programme running. The push for modularisation didn't how-ever come from the CNAA. Instead the issue of modularisation became the subject of a contentious debate between those who objected to its lack of coherence and specialisation and those who favoured and argued for its flexibility and accessibility. By 1986 Theodossin (p28) concluded that, 'intellectually valid or not, the conviction that modular courses lack coherence is by now deeply embedded in the educational culture'.

And yet by 1994 virtually all of the former polytechnics have now adopted a modular approach whilst only a few of the older universities have shown virtually no interest in converting. So much for embeddedness.

It seems that the contentious debate of the 1970's and 1980's which appeared to have rejected modularisation as lacking coherence has now been won by its proponents on grounds of accessibility and flexibility. No doubt economic and especially funding pressures have contributed to this change in attitude. And no doubt too the state will continue to pressurise higher education institutions. In order that universities and colleges should be more responsive to student demand, credit accumulation and transfer coupled with modularisation will be pushed hard to facilitate flows of students both between and within higher education institutions.

But the universities have not actually been forced into it. The former polytechnics may well have seized upon modularisation in order to gain a competitive advantage over their more traditional rivals. But these, with few exceptions, are now also adopting modularisation for the same reasons which include both market-led considerations and the more socially-related benefits of access and flexibility. Indeed were modularisation to be forced on the universities then it would be unlikely to succeed for 'coercive changes, particularly when they conflict with strongly held internal norms, are inherently unstable. They are implemented, if at all, under a sense of duress, with its attendant overtures of resentment, rejection and, in some cases, moral outrage' (Becher and Kogan 1992, p138). There has been a certain amount of resentment at the introduction of modularisation in the UK. But the general argument appears to have been won despite the problems of implementation. The main thing is to make it work for the benefit of students and society.

Aren't modules actually about improving general education, and isn't HE actually about specialisation? 19

Modules themselves are simply part of a delivery system which differs from the traditional one. Their impact, in terms of specialist or general education , is entirely neutral.

Modular systems are a different matter. Most modular systems incorporate a lot of choice for students. In setting up the framework for choice, system designers can choose to compel specialisation by requiring that a large proportion of modules must be chosen from within named fields of study, or they can compel diversification by putting limits on the number of modules students are allowed to choose from within specialist areas, or they can leave it very much up to the students.

So modular systems can be about encouraging specialisation, or about encouraging diversification, or about striking a compromise between the two. The larger and more flexible schemes can, in fact, be so designed as to met the needs of a wide range of students, and to adapt fairly easily to changing patterns of demand. At Anglia Polytechnic University, for example, a shift in demand in a particular academic area, from Single Honours to Combined Honours, was absorbed without any need to modify course structures or administrative procedures.

It seems to be the case, therefore, that modular systems can be so designed as to be much more responsive to changing and/or varied needs than is possible in more traditional structures. But they will only do this successfully if they are carefully designed with that purpose in mind.

Can modular systems cope with the demands of professional courses? 20

Modular systems can cope with most things, so long as they have been carefully designed to do so. The better ones do in fact manage to cope with the different needs of varied groups of students reasonably well.

As we have stated elsewhere, one of the features of large modular schemes is the amount of freedom most of them give for students to make choices within their programme of study. In the scheme the authors know best, for example, a student makes choices at a number of levels.

The initial choice is between a Single or a Combined Honours programme.

Next comes the choice of main subject (one or two). This choice imposes the requirement that two thirds of the Year One programme, and three quarters of the Years Two and Three programme, must be chosen from within the main subject(s). Generally speaking, within each subject there will be a choice of modules available, so that the student can meet this requirement in a number of different ways.

The remaining modules can be chosen from any subject offered within the scheme, not excluding the main subject(s). Thus the student can choose, with advice from academic staff, either to broaden his/her programme through complementary studies, or to deepen the study of the main subject(s).

Whilst no two modular schemes are exactly alike, most would offer similar levels of choice.

The difficulty comes in reconciling this degree of choice with the requirements of professional bodies, many of which are fairly prescriptive of course content. This has led some institutions to exempt professional courses from modularity.

Other institutions have taken the view that it is desirable to incorporate professional courses into their modular scheme if at all possible, so as to achieve the economies which can be gained through module sharing and, from a more purely educational point of view, to open up to other students access to modules in those areas of study.

Solutions adopted in those institutions include exempting professional programmes from some of the basic ground rules of the scheme if they can demonstrate that a professional body's requirements make this necessary; definition of some modules (in some circumstances, almost all modules) as compulsory for students aiming for professional accreditation (they can remain optional for other students); or a combination of the two approaches.

Chapter 3
Staff and student questions

21 Aren't staff and students confused by modules?
22 Does modularisation offer students too much choice or too little choice?
23 If modularisation is about choice then how can that choice be well-informed?
24 Do modules really encourage active or deep learning?
25 How are modules best delivered?
26 Don't modules lead to over-assessment?
27 How are modules best assessed?
28 Does modularisation really foster change and innovation?
29 Don't modular programmes make extra demands on support staff?
30 Don't modules just make life simpler for the educational accountant and harder for everyone else?
31 Don't modular programmes lead to mixed ability groups which most university teachers can't really handle?
32 How are modules best evaluated?

Aren't staff and students confused by modules?   21

There is some evidence, that students are confused about the new modular systems. UK students, unlike American students, have not had since 1869 to get used to what has been cruelly described as 'educational banking par excellence' (Barnett 1994).

And the students are not alone. Many staff in higher education are also confused. They get confused with the proliferating terminology of modularity. University modular schemes already spawn their own jargon: sets, fields, levels, strands, pathways, infield, outfield, major entry principle and defined module variants to name but a few. These all seemed necessary and desirable at the time but, despite the obvious good intentions of their authors, have duly added to the confusion.

The confusion is compounded by what staff see as too much paper work and too much administration. The trouble is that modularity has been introduced at the same time, in many higher education institutions, as an increase in student numbers. Thus the problems due to more students are seen to be associated with modularity.

Students and staff are confused because they perceive a deterioration in the quality of their professional relationships and they put this down to the introduction of modularity. Staff complain that they can't get to know students in the short time available, that students no longer enjoy their studies and just prepare for the assessment. Staff are beginning to feel less job satisfaction because they now face huge banks of nameless students. Staff are often irritated by what they see as the imposition of modularity.

The evidence available is that staff and students are confused and frustrated by the way modularity has been introduced and implemented. However despite the obsession with assessment staff often think that a modular system gives students a clear picture of what is expected of them and that it has also made relevance and applicability clearer.

So students and staff are to an extent confused by modules. This is hardly surprising given that a massive change in the way in which teaching and learning are delivered in our universities and colleges has taken place, for the most part, over a relatively short period of time. The confusion stems mainly from the relative newness of the approach as well as from mistakes in its introduction and initial implementation. Given careful and continuous review and, perhaps, a move to semesters, much of this confusion might eventually be dispelled.

The confusion might be dispelled by offering students fuller descriptions of what modules contain and what outcomes are intended, by guiding and counselling students through the new terminology and procedures entailed by prerequisites and corequisites, fields and pathways and by providing staff with opportunities (through staff handbooks and staff development activities) to increase their understanding of the new system and its processes. This does not, however, move us away from the metaphor of education as banking so criticised by Barnett in his attack on the increasing fragmentation and operationalism of higher education.

Does modularisation offer students too much choice or too little choice? 22

Anyone who has seen the undergraduate catalogue of most American colleges or universities is presented with a vast array of courses or modules. Anyone new to the system could feel overwhelmed by so much choice in so many subject areas. For example in one catalogue immediately to hand there are over 1600 first and second year modules in over 90 subject areas. The subjects include the *academic* e.g. Anthropology, Art, Astronomy to Zoology, and the *vocational* e.g. Aeronautical Sciences, Allied Health, Automotive Technology to Water Technology and Welding. Although UK universities tend to be smaller than their US counterparts the modular offerings have proliferated. In some UK universities there are now over 4500 validated modules in their developing modular schemes. Thus it appears that there is a lot of choice in the system, perhaps too much.

Again, however, appearances are deceptive. US colleges and universities, having created choice, have also set up mechanisms which restrict choice and flexibility (see 11 above) by for example insisting on

- *requirements*
    - for English and Mathematics and to meet General Education requirements by taking modules from each teaching area such as Humanities, Sciences and Social Sciences
- *prerequisites*
    - especially for those wishing to major in a particular subject

- *corequisites*
    - in order to provide coherence or sufficient specialisation for a major.

The UK has also learned to restrict choice by using a similar range of mechanisms including those just referred to as well as *level* restrictions, *sets, exclusion* and *non-availability* (see 11 above).

Thus any one modular scheme can produce abundant choice or restricted choice. The more we wish to retain the specialist nature of the UK's undergraduate programmes the more likely it is that we will restrict choice. The more we wish to provide a broader more flexible first degree programme the more choice we shall build into the system.

If modularisation is about student choice 23 then how can that choice be well-informed?

Modularisation is certainly about a degree of student choice. So how can students be helped to become informed consumers of what we deliver? (We leave aside here the point made above in answer to question 10 that students are better envisaged as at least co-deliverers of their own modular learning).

Informing students about choice in modular courses is rapidly following the traditional US pattern. Catalogues, often computer-based, are being produced which summarise what each module is about. In most cases students should be able to access each Module Reference Sheet which should give them a full picture of each module's prerequisites and corequisites, if any, its learning outcomes, delivery method, learning activities, assessment requirements, outline content and indicative learning resources.

However apart from all this practical detail students need to be informed about a whole range of other issues. In American Community Colleges, for example, students need to know about university transfer requirements so that they can plan their college programme in order

- to select an education/career goal
- to select an appropriate major to meet that goal
- to select a college or university
- to develop and complete an appropriate course of study in preparation for transfer.

Students in American colleges and universities are encouraged to consult an adviser in a Counselling or Transfer Centre in order to get clear information about, especially, preparation for taking a major.

In our own systems in the UK many students say that there is insufficient pre-course guidance to enable them to take full advantage of modular schemes. Students complain of complex and out-of-date procedures and the need for more user-friendly documentation. Suggestions for improvement include midterm module fairs, comprehensive field guide booklets, pre-sessional study skills sessions and more guidance to mature students to prevent culture shock. Students want course and module advice at Faculty level and welfare, finance, accommodation, student records and administration provided centrally. A full, central, computerised, information system is really required to support complete modularisation. However much of the advice and counselling that students need in the UK is currently sought from subject or module leaders who may not be in the best position to offer impartial advice about particular modules or programmes. In the UK we shall have to become a lot more professional in our provision of counselling services for modular programmes. Fortunately this is already beginning to happen in a much more systematic way especially in relation to advice and guidance or, for example, the accreditation of prior learning and on the transfer of credits between higher education institutions. But we don't believe there is much room for complacency.

Do modules really encourage active or deep learning? 24

Does teaching in higher education encourage active or deep learning? Sadly, it seems that the only people who actually use terms such an 'deep' or 'surface' learning in any regular way are those who have a professional interest in their use - often researchers in teaching and learning in higher education and various higher education staff developers. 'Deep' and 'surface' are regularly heard at Staff and Educational Development Association (SEDA) conferences but not very often, we suspect, in the staffrooms of our universities and colleges.

Deep' and 'surface' are approaches to learning. A 'surface' approach is one where students learn to memorise and reproduce a set of (unconnected) facts about a topic or subject for later use, especially for regurgitation in an examination. A 'deep' approach is one where students attempt to learn how to make sense of a topic or subject by seeking an integration of its ideas and concepts. The crucial difference between the two approaches is whether students *search for meaning* during their learning tasks, whether they are *active* in trying to understand a topic or *passive* in trying to reproduce its facts.

Modules can encourage either deep or surface approaches to learning. One module could simply encourage students just to learn a set of unconnected facts about a topic - it would thus encourage a surface approach to learning. Another module could encourage students to learn a set of important facts as they relate to the key concepts of a topic : 'surface is, at best, about quantity without quality; deep is about quality and quantity' (Ramsden 1992 p45). Of course, students need to 'learn' some things right now in order that the 'meaning' will develop later. The danger is that module designers will cram their modules with too much content and pay too little attention to those important learning outcomes which relate to meaning and understanding.

It's up to us : we can design and deliver our modules in such a way that students come *to adopt a search for understanding and connection* (with e.g. previous knowledge, with other modules, between theory and practice, between argument and evidence) or in such a way that students merely come to *complete the requirements of the task or the assessment* (by only focusing on unrelated parts and facts, by treating tasks as external impositions, by failing to distinguish between argument and evidence).

Modules can obviously be designed and delivered which encourage students to collect and regurgitate facts. They can also be designed and delivered in a way which helps them search for meaning and understanding of important concepts and principles. Presumably we want understanding and meaning even if, all too often, we settle for facts.

How are modules best delivered? 25

It all depends on what we want. If we want meaning and understanding (see items 3,5,7) then we will deliver our modules according to one set of criteria. If we want an accumulation of facts we shall deliver our modules according to a different set.

Assuming that the modules we want to deliver will seek to encourage meaning and understanding, how are such modules best delivered?

We believe that module delivery which encourages meaning and understanding will *get students fully involved in planning their own learning, stimulate active teaching and learning processes, enable learning to take place within dynamic interactive group settings and help students to relate new subject-matter to their existing knowledge and experience.*

Getting students fully involved in planning their learning progress in any particular module requires that the tutor discusses and clarifies the module's learning outcomes, learning activities, assessments, content and key learning resources as soon and as thoroughly as possible with the students. The danger here is that students may only see what is required of them for assessment purposes. Tutors need to emphasise that the overall teaching/learning process is as important as the delivery of subject content if the student is to achieve meaning and understanding.

Active and interactive teaching and learning could be encouraged if tutors adopt the guide to good practice adapted from the recent Wingspread Report on Higher Education in the USA:

Seven principles of good practice in student learning

1 Good practice encourages *student-teacher contact*
2 Good practice promotes *cooperation among students*
3 Good practice encourages *active learning*

4   Good practice requires *prompt feedback*
5   Good practice demands *prime time on each main learning task*
6   Good practice depends on *high expectations*
7   Good practice respects *diverse talents and ways of learning.*

(adapted from Wingspread 1993).

The change to a modular system means that we in the UK run the risk of further reducing student-teacher contact, encouraging more competition rather than cooperation amongst students, producing passivity rather than activity in our classes, emphasising summative assessment rather than regular formative feedback, pushing main learning tasks away from prime time for students, lowering our demands and expectations and implying that modularity requires uniformity in outcomes and standardisation of approach.

Further, if we fail to deliver our modules according to these seven principles, or to a similar set, we shall also, quite probably, fail to help students develop a more structured understanding of each module's subject content. For we do know that meaning and understanding require that students, for example, need contact with mature learners (such as their tutors), need to discuss and check out their understanding of concepts and ideas with other students, need to get prompt feedback if they are to progress and need to be challenged into producing good quality work.

Thus modules are best delivered by teachers acting on good principles of teaching and learning in order to achieve meaning and understanding in their students.

Don't modules lead to over-assessment?　　26

In the good old days students had a set of exams at the end of their first year and then another set, finals, at the end of their third year. Nobody then complained of over-assessment. The main complaints were about the apparent lack of challenge in the second year and the over-reliance on summative assessment procedures, particularly three hour unseen examinations which tested memory rather than understanding.

Under a modular system where students may be required to take 36 modules over a three year period there is a danger that, where each module is individually assessed, too much pressure is put on students and staff by the assessment process. In effect full-time students may be faced with four major assessments per term in order to meet the demands of the system.

The good thing about all this is that students should get regular and continuous assessment throughout their programme. The bad thing is that students (and staff) come to feel that their work is driven by summative assessment procedures rather than informed and improved by clear feedback and formative assessment processes.

The evidence from the modular scheme at Oxford Brookes University is that initially staff seized the opportunity to move away from the final unseen examination as the major form of assessment to a much more varied selection of coursework assessments such as essays, reports, group projects and oral presentations (see Gibbs and Jenkins 1992 p33).

However the pressure caused by larger groups has meant that many staff feel overwhelmed by the volume of marking required so that they have again resorted to the final unseen examination or the use of coursework which is easy to mark. Even here, however, they are faced with the problem of having to develop new skills and new materials in order to use multiple-choice questions or computer-based marking.

So modules can lead to over-assessment and can also lead us back to rather conservative methods of summative assessment. The worrying move away from formative coursework assessment is linked to a move away from important educational practices such as discussion, counselling, advising and debriefing which always seemed both necessary and desirable with small groups of 10 to 15 students but which now seem impossible with groups of 30 to 40 students.

One solution to the problem is for staff teams to adopt a *strategic approach to assessment* of modules which involves planning a *variety of assessments* including, if necessary, both seen and unseen examinations and non-essay examinations throughout a student's programme. This requires that individual module designers are brought up against the reality of seeing their modules in the context of various pathways or programmes which must feature different ways of assessing different learning outcomes.

We could attempt to avoid over-assessment of our modular programmes by adopting the following seven basic strategies:

- realising the limits of assessment
- avoiding over-questioning and over-sampling
- involving students in the process through
  - joint design of questions and assessment criteria
  - joint selection of assessment methods including self- and peer-assessment
- providing positive and corrective feedback on key issues only
- focusing on valid assessments of the students' understanding rather than their memories
- making assessment more criterion-referenced than norm-referenced
- grouping modules for assessment purposes

(based on Ramsden 1992 and Andresen 1993).

How are modules best assessed? 27

We have already suggested that a *strategic approach to assessment* of modules which involves planning *a variety of assessments* is possibly the best way of avoiding over-assessment. We also think that a strategic approach which includes a repertoire of assessment methods is an appropriate way to begin the process of selecting the best ways to assess modules.

Again, however, we need to think very clearly about *the purposes of assessment, the validity and reliability of the methods and processes used, the practicability of assessing modules, the criteria of assessment used, how assessment can also deliver feedback to students, the variety and amount of assessment and the need to be free of bias.*

When we examine the specific *purposes of assessment* in particular modules or courses we obviously need to examine a number of important questions. For example, if we are interested in encouraging deep approaches to learning, we will attempt to assess skills and competences which indicate understanding of key ideas, concepts and principles. We will need to ask whether, for instance, a 2000-word essay is the best assessment task for students to demonstrate, and for us to judge, their understanding of those key ideas.

Obviously we need to be clear that the assessment methods and system chosen really do assess what we want to assess.

Overall we need to be sure that when we assess a module we are seeking to use specific assessment tasks for *particular assessment purposes* which could include, for example, the following:

Purposes of assessment
- To provide feedback to students to improve their learning
- To motivate students

- To diagnose students' strengths and weaknesses
- To help students to develop their skills of self assessment
- To provide a profile of what a student has learnt
- To pass or fail a student
- To grade or rank a student
- To licence to proceed
- To select for future courses
- To licence to practice
- To predict success in future courses
- To predict success in employment
- To select for future employment
- To provide feedback to lecturers
- To motivate lecturers
- To evaluate a course's strengths and weaknesses
- To make the course appear 'respectable' and creditworthy to other institutions and employers

(from Brown and Pendlebury 1992 p9).

The important issue here is to ensure that the assessment tasks chosen will serve the particular set of purposes we have identified.

A second group of issues relates to the *validity and reliability* of the methods used. *Validity* is often defined in terms of the closeness or accuracy of the match between what is intended to be assessed and what is actually assessed. A module will have valid assessment methods and procedures in so far as there is a close match between its intended learning outcomes (e.g. particular skills or competences) and the assessment tasks used. In effect validity is a test of fitness of purpose : the 2000-word essay is meant to be a valid test of the student's ability to present a case, say, for or against, a particular assertion or claim in history or economics or literature. In such an instance the essay may be regarded as both *appropriate* and *valid* in testing the particular purpose of diagnosing a student's strengths and weaknesses in writing history, economics, literary criticism or whatever. *Reliability* is more a question of whether assessment is consistent between markers or assessors. Would, for example, two assessors come to the same conclusion about a student's essay? Would the same assessors come to the same conclusions about the same essay a few day's later?

For modules to be both validly and reliably assessed, therefore, staff have first to justify that they are actually measuring what they set out to measure and, second, to show that they are being as consistent and objective as possible in the assessment process.

Unfortunately the arrival of modules in higher education has also led to an increase in staff workload so that staff have often felt overwhelmed by the demands of the new assessment requirements. Students may also feel over-assessed. As a result the usual solutions to improving assessment- involving students in the assessment process through greater use of self- and peer-assessment and through joint design of tasks and assessment criteria, making assessment more criterion-referenced than norm-refer- enced, seeing assessment as feedback, promoting tutor reliability and using more double-marking - may not seem immediately *practicable*.

Nevertheless we believe that modules are best assessed when staff do adopt, as far as is practicable, the seven basic strategies referred to above in item 26. We obviously need to select from a much broader repertoire of assessment methods in order to avoid the monotony of always using the same kinds of assessment tasks to serve a limited range of assessment purposes. Fortunately much more help is now available to enable staff to select from a much more appropriate and valid set of assessment tasks to meet some of the more interesting assessment purposes required of students including, for example,
* assessing *practical work*
* assessing *projects*
* assessing *problem-solving*
* assessing *work-based learning*
* assessing *oral communication*

- assessing *group work*
- assessing *Enterprise learning.*

Assessment should not be restricted to the three-hour written examination or the 3000 word essay. Also, the *amount* of assessment should also be appropriate. Unfortunately module designers and module deliverers often feel that their particular modules are undervalued or less worthy if they are not assessed by, for example, a 3000 word essay.

The timing of assessment is also an important issue. Most American teachers plan a series of formative assessments including quizzes, multiple choice questions and short answer questions during their courses or modules and then conclude with a more formal term paper as a summative assessment. Hard-pressed UK university teachers, who tend to teach four to five modules per term compared with two to three per term or semester in the USA, may well feel that one summative assessment per module is enough especially with increasing class sizes. However one important feature of all modular systems is that assessment is carried out during or immediately on completion of each module. And once a module is completed and assessed students are not required to be tested on its content or outcomes again. They are not required, as used to be the case in traditional university courses, to carry forward first and second year learning to be assessed as part of their final year examinations.

And, finally, we also believe that modules are best assessed in as unbiased a way as possible. This may require each university or college for example to screen assessment tasks for gender or racial bias, to use candidate numbers rather than names in exams and to respect diversity and differences in learning styles by providing a broad range of assessment tasks in each modular programme.

Does modularisation really foster change and innovation? 28

The simple answer to this question is, probably, no. Modularisation is a neutral device for curricular accounting which can be packed with stale content which is delivered conventionally and unenterprisingly. However modularisation doesn't preclude change and innovation and has in many cases stimulated staff in higher education to think of different ways of designing and delivering their programme.

Perhaps the best early example of modularisation stimulating change and innovation was provided by the Open University in the 1970's Some of us who were in higher education at that time became involved as part-time tutors just in order to be part of the climate of innovation and enterprise and were impressed by the way in which OU course units were designed using subject specialists *and* educational technologists so that the twin issues of subject content and learning process were considered and dealt with jointly. The result was the production of course units which, though not perfect, had clear objectives, set interesting tasks, used well-produced and attractive materials and utilised radio and TV to introduce a mainly non-traditional and mature student population to study in higher education.

Modules can, of course, be designed which are no more than fragments of traditional programmes and which show that little effort has been made to meet the learning needs of students in anything other than a perfunctory way. However, a trawl of the modules on offer in any university will indicate examples of exciting change and innovation.

At Oxford Brookes, for instance, a new compulsory double module in social work sought to harness student effort creatively to enable them to tackle issues relating to groups, discrimination and empowerment. The module was mainly delivered in small, task centred groups of six students who were required to investigate and report on the extent and consequences of discrimination for a client group and to work with some of those so discriminated against in order to identify one achievable improvement. Students learned about one area of discrimination through their own group's investigation and about other areas through the presentations of peer groups. Each group graded its own work and that of the other groups and the module's two lecturers also provided their grades which carried a similar weight. Students also had to write an individual paper describing and evaluating the group process, a task aided by the requirement to keep a diary and submit a bibliography. Students learned how to negotiate with their peers to achieve their aims, to agree areas of responsibility, to define problems and to seek answers. Overall the module was characterised by high motivation and good attendance. The group presentation showed evidence of hard self-directed work and learning as well as increased student confidence and decisive action with respect to issues of discrimination relating for example to HIV/AIDS and to ethnic minorities. The end result was that the students' knowledge about groups, discrimination and empowerment is thorough, almost certainly because of the experiential learning (Gillies 1993).

At Anglia Polytechnic University one innovation which has had a significant impact on in-service students is the module on Comparative Education in the European Context. This module was designed as a component of a part-time Certificate course for teachers in Post-Compulsory Education to enable them to examine and reflect upon educational and professional issues in Europe with particular reference to pedagogical approaches, educational systems, resource mechanisms, assumptions about learning, and about assessment and evaluation. Some context and background are provided by the module tutor but the main feature of the module is either a study visit to an EU member state or an individual project. A small grant of £100 is offered to each student who chooses his/her own individually-negotiated study visit. The notion of negotiation is crucial. First, the student has to negotiate with his/her own department and college to gain the necessary one week's release in order to undertake the visit. Not all students are successful at this stage mainly because of resource problems in their own colleges. Second, the student has to negotiate and plan his/her own study visit by contacting colleges abroad. Sometimes this is facilitated by their own college's overseas links and sometimes through the university's own contacts. Finally, the students have to negotiate their way through their visits using a variety of interpersonal and diplomatic skills and then submit a 2000 word report as part of the module's assessment requirements. Students who undertake this study visit option attest to its impact on them as a learning experience particularly as, in most cases, they have often gained their posts in further education as a result of work experience and part-time study and have not enjoyed the advantages of periods of full-time study let alone even a small sample of study abroad. For many the study visit is an illuminating experience and represents, so they say, a high point and even a turning-point in their professional lives in terms of generating new knowledge, cultural learning and personal development.

Modularity can be such a flexible device that it can offer alert departments the chance of seizing opportunities when they arise. During 1993-94 the Department of Education at Anglia was able to encourage an American professor of sociology to design a module on Current Issues in American Education before she arrived for a term's secondment so that she could deliver the module during the summer term of 1994. The department was able to organise the module's validation and to advertise its intended outcomes and indicative content to prospective students during the autumn and spring terms of 1993-94. The in-service students drawn from primary, secondary and further education were able to experience a module designed and delivered by an American professor which covered topics such as development and change in the curriculum and its relationship to society, family and school links, the problem of violence in schools and the nature of the assessment process. In this case the innovation comprised the comparative nature of the topics covered, the American flavour of the learning materials used and the particular teaching style of the visiting professor. Anglia's students received an innovative experience mainly as a result of the opportunity the American's presence offered.

Modules can and do foster change and innovation. But, of course, they won't if we use them as mere containers of old educational materials.

Don't modular programmes make extra demands on support staff? 29

The American evidence is that modular programmes can't be run efficiently and effectively unless they are well-supported by a broad range of support staff. These include, in British parlance, modular scheme coordinators or directors, admissions staff, guidance staff, administrative and secretarial staff, library staff, information systems staff, media production staff, computing staff and finance staff.

For example Anglia has now appointed two coordinators of the university modular scheme. In effect they manage the scheme and chair many of its working parties and committees. They co-chair the University Modular System's (UMS) Steering Group which itself sets up various Liaison Groups which 'progress the detailed work associated with the operationalisation of UMS'. These Liaison Groups, which the UMS Coordinators also chair, include ones dedicated to Admissions and Recruitment, Timetabling, Academic Counselling and Personal Tutoring, Assessment and Administration Procedures. All groups include substantial representation from support staff from, for example, Student Administration, Student Services, Management Information Services, Marketing and International Relations. Most support service staff are interested in being involved in planning the modular system but the committee and group work have placed extra demands on their time and energy.

Support staff in computing, library and media production areas are also facing considerable extra demands both on their own time and on the resources at their disposal. Some of this extra demand results from the increase in student numbers over the past five years but some of it is owing to the change to modularisation. These staff have continuously sought clarification and assurances about the apparent increased resource demands made by the modular curriculum. They are concerned, for example, that resources, particularly in IT, which have hitherto been owned by individual departments and faculties will *not* become part of a university-wide provision following the move to a university-wide modular system. They think there will be extra demands at particular times for specific resources (especially in IT) which they will be unable to meet. An increase in Foundation studies modules will inevitably lead to large groups of students demanding high levels of support from library, computing and media staff all at the same time. Similarly the greater use of assessment by project or dissertation which modularity often favours also makes greater learning resource demands on service areas. Increase in the numbers of associate students also has considerable implications since they tend to make disproportionate demands on resources in relation to the income they generate.

These extra demands on support staff come on top of the familiar litany of complaints relating to increased numbers of students in higher education :

- fewer books per student
- students unable to afford books
- narrower range of books
- single copies of reference sources
- less reading and less relevant reading
- narrow reading and more predictable essays
- discouragement of reading and use of libraries

(see Bluck et al 1994, p21).

Two strategies could be adopted to tackle these complaints : a control strategy and an independence strategy (see Gibbs 1991). The *control strategy* requires more set books and learning packages (which again take time and money) but tends to ignore the library as a core resource. The *independence strategy* requires a development of students' research skills to enable them to find more varied sources for the essays and projects particularly in collaboration with the university library and its information networks. Library managers, (see Bluck et al 1994, p22), need 'to embrace a genuine strategic role for information skills' which would enable library staff to meet the 'exponential increase in demand' brought about, we think, by a combination of greater student numbers, the information explosion and the change to modularity. Libraries and other support staff may also, in order to be proactive in the face of the exponential increase in demand, have to become more innovative in their approach to user education. For example at De Montfort University the library has established a Student Learning Development Centre which helps students develop the skills and abilities to cope with changes in teaching and learning as well as to disseminate student centred learning materials.

Modern teaching and learning approaches (including modular courses) require buildings which can accommodate both silent study groups and noisy (interactive) working groups. Student based learning, which is more and more a feature of modularity, places greater stress on the physical resources of the library (which we now call a learning resources centre) including better and different access to learning materials. This inevitably leads to demands for 24 hour access and study facilities which is already a feature of many US campuses.

Modularity does make extra demands on support staff as these references to the library service show. These extra demands include the need for extra staff for development work, the reorganisation of the library for non-traditional working, an expansion of study space and facilities for remote access.

Don't modules just make life simpler for the educational accountant and harder for everyone else? 30

It is arguable that, far from making life easier for the accountants and administrators, modularity actually complicates their lives enormously.

Traditional courses have the great virtue that students are clearly, in most cases, based in a particular department, which looks after all aspects of their programme. This makes devolved financial management relatively simple to operate, and makes the task of central administrative units also quite simple, in that they can receive information about each student from a single source.

Modularity changes this. In large and complex modular schemes, students' programmes are quite likely to straddle departmental or faculty boundaries. This complicates accounting processes, and requires sophisticated central systems to keep track of credits accumulated by the students. The task is not impossible, since modules generally can be defined as a proportion of a year's work. But it is complex.

Modularity also brings changes for academic staff. They are less likely to get to know their students well, since schemes with choice built in can produce student groups which vary greatly between different modules within the same subject. At the same time, students in modular schemes require higher levels of advice and guidance on their choice of modules, compared to those on more prescriptive traditional courses.

So in many senses, modularity makes life more difficult all round for staff.

On the other hand, those who have worked in large modular schemes frequently report that 'modular students' are often better motivated, more mature in their attitude to their courses (which they have had a hand in shaping) and tend to achieve better results. Many staff are prepared to say that these benefits outweigh the negative aspects.

In the end , it seems to us to be a question of how far one considers that the creation of greater flexibility in course structures justifies abandoning some of the features (cohort identity, strong relationships between teachers and taught, etc.) which have in the past been felt to characterise HE.

Don't modular programmes lead to mixed ability groups which most university teachers can't really handle? 31

To the extent that modular schemes allow students to enrol for modules outside their main area of study, it is clearly the case that a particular module is likely to contain both subject specialists and students who are simply broadening their programme. Some HE lecturers will regard this as a problem.

There are, however, ways in which the 'problem', if problem it be, can be minimised.

Firstly, it is clearly essential that the scheme contain robust means of determining the level of each module, and ensuring that the level does not slip under pressure from non-specialists.

Provided this is in place, the rest depends on a combination of effective advice to students, so that they do not enrol for modules with which they would have difficulty coping, and a system of prerequisites to ensure that students cannot take, for example, Nuclear Physics 2 if they have not achieved the learning outcomes of Nuclear Physics 1.

Having said this, we cannot resist adding that, in any case, teaching mixed ability groups ought not, in the last analysis, to be more difficult for university teachers than for other kinds of teacher. The right response to the 'problem' of mixed ability teaching might be a requirement for university teachers to have undertaken initial training and/or Staff Development, rather than restricting student choice.

How are modules best evaluated? 32

We start with the assumption that course and module evaluation is mainly about *improvement*. Evaluation in this sense should be for the university, its staff, its students and other stakeholders to enable them to judge, overall, whether or not a particular module or course is of an excellent or satisfactory or unsatisfactory standard. If a module is unsatisfactory the university should be able to use the evaluation data collected to formulate an action plan for its improvement. If a module is satisfactory then the evaluation data should be used to clarify why it is so in order to ensure that this acceptable standard is maintained and, if possible, improved. And if a module is judged to be excellent then, after the celebrations, the excellent features should be made public as quickly as possible lest they be forgotten or ignored.

However as with good design or good teaching or good assessment there is no one best way of conducting evaluations of courses or modules. Indeed there are dozens of approaches ranging from Action Research, Action Evaluation and Autocratic Evaluation to Systems Analysis, Utilisation-Focused Evaluation and Zero-based Budgeting.

O'Neill and Pennington recommend that higher education teachers develop an evaluation strategy which represents an agreed group (teaching group, group of module tutors, course team) approach and which enables them to clarify:
- the *purposes* of their course or module evaluation
- individual *responsibilities* and involvements
- *focus* - on which aspects of the module or course?
- *sources of data*
- *means for gathering data*
- *policies and procedures* - especially when and how often and for whom?
(see O'Neill and Pennington 1992, pp53-54).

We favour an *illuminative approach to evaluation* (see Parlett and Hamilton 1976) which attempts to *describe* and *interpret* an educational project (such as a module or course) rather than *measure* its products or *predict* its outcomes. Illuminative evaluation tries to study the actual operation of a module or course especially through the perceptions of its main participants - the tutors themselves and their students. Illuminative evaluation aims to discover and document what it is like to be a participant in a module or course and to discern and discuss its most significant features and critical processes. It is therefore an adaptable and eclectic strategy which is focused on both the *'instructional system'* or how the module/course is delivered and the broader *'learning milieu'*. Illuminative evaluation deliberately attends to the broad context in which the module takes place and equally deliberately

- respects the *perceptions* of those involved
- uses a variety of *sources* for collecting data
- uses a variety of *data-collection methods*
- encourages a variety of ways of producing evaluative *reports*.

Evaluating the module as an *'instructional system'* will focus on whether the module's intended learning *objectives or outcomes* have been achieved, whether the *content* was relevant and interesting to the students, whether the *teaching, learning* and *assessment* methods were appropriate and whether the module's *resources* (including staff) were adequate and suitable. An illuminative evaluation will also seek to discover whether the broader 'learning milieu' was also appropriate for the particular module or course under scrutiny.

Feedback data for an illuminative evaluation would be sought from a number of sources but most especially from the students themselves, academic staff and other significant stakeholders (not excluding university administrators, external assessors, and workplace supervisors). All of these stakeholders have interests in the evaluation which are both *summative* - in that they want to come to some conclusion about the module's satisfactoriness - and *formative* - in that they want to contribute to change and improvement.

We think that students are the most important sources of feedback data and that they should be encouraged through the use of a *variety of methods of collecting data* to make a major contribution to the evaluation process. Illuminative evaluation draws from an eclectic array of data-collection methods including :

- student questionnaires
- course questionnaires
- staff questionnaires
- group discussions, workshops and conferences
- interviews with staff and students
- diaries, journals and logbooks kept by staff and students
- portfolios of other relevant documentation such as module handbooks and examples of teaching and learning materials
- students' creative work
- memos and letters
- examples of critical incidents.

Most of these are familiar techniques for collecting feedback and they represent a repertoire of methods from which module evaluators could select. More often than not, given the time and resource constraints we now face, evaluators will probably select only one or two methods for use. In the USA, for example, each course is virtually evaluated by student questionnaire only, a process which is deemed to be objective, cheap and effective

However caution is needed in the use of student ratings of staff since they ought to be collected impartially and not by the teaching staff themselves, to be based on a representative sample of students from each class, to be distributed and collected under prescribed conditions and to be collected on every member of staff. It is not known whether any UK universities conform to these conditions . The danger is that student questionnaires will be used to assess teachers whereas what we are more interested in is evaluating the satisfactoriness or otherwise of modules and courses. Ramsden's Course Evaluation Questionnaire (see Ramsden 1992 Appendix) attempts, instead, to provide a direct measure of consumer/student satisfaction with their course. We think its 30 questions could be used by hard pressed module leaders to collect data on, preferably, groups of modules or courses rather than individual modules as such.

A simpler way of getting feedback on any individual module is Gibbs's 'Structured Group Feedback' method which Ramsden also describes and which is based on the teacher asking the class to write down their answers to three questions:

1   What was the BEST feature of this module for you?
2   What was the WORST feature of this module for you?
3   In what ways do you think the module could be improved?

Students can be asked to discuss their responses in groups of four and then have their agreed comments collated by the teacher in front of the class. Each group could report on 'best feature' which could be checked with the other groups to see if they agree. Agreed 'best' and 'worst' features and 'improvements' could then be compared with the teacher's own perceptions of the module's strengths and weaknesses. The important evaluative point here is to treat student feedback as valuable data and not as a requirement to agree with what students claim they want. Evaluation requires judgement, not compliance.

Some of the data collection methods will be more appropriate for certain modules rather than others. Diaries, journals and logbooks are particularly suitable for collecting data from research-based modules or work-experience modules where the data may be used for both assessment and evaluation purposes. Students' creative work is a vital source of data, again for both assessment and evaluation, for modules in the arts fields.

How module or course evaluation should be *reported* is an interesting question. Most reports for quality assurance purposes would tend to be brief and would emphasise feedback data about, mainly, student satisfaction with the course. Reporting on a course could, however, be regarded as a piece of action research for students and staff particularly where the keeping of a log or diary or journal offers students (or staff) the opportunity of noting the raw data of experience so that it becomes an *aide memoire* for an account of what they felt like as participants in the module's delivery processes. This requires that students go beyond mere data-collection to the more educationally-rewarding and fulfilling processes of clarification, assimilation and reflection.

Illuminative evaluation of modules and courses can encourage students not only to become participants in the module or course delivery process but also, in partnership with their tutors, involved in, and integrated with, the evaluation process itself. And this too will add yet another important skill as a learning outcome to their modular course.

Chapter 4
Semesters

Technical questions

33　What are semesters - surely not another trendy American import?

34　How long are semesters?

35　When should the academic year start?

36　So what did Flowers recommend?

37　How long do you need between semesters?

38　What is the 'third semester'?

39　Won't the change from terms to semesters be unmanageable?

40　Do semester dates need to be the same at all universities?

What are semesters - surely not another   33 trendy American import?

Semester ought to mean 'a period of six months'. By the same token, a trimester, or term, ought to be three months long.

In practice, of course, 'term' generally describes the study period in systems which divide the academic year into three sessions - though in the US. the word 'quarter' may be more common; semester has come to be used to describe the study period in systems which divide the academic year into two sessions.

Semesters are often thought to be an American idea. In fact, they are by no means universal in the USA, where some universities deal in quarters, are very common in mainland Europe, and are gaining in popularity in the UK. Quarters, not surprisingly, come in fours, but one, the Summer quarter, is usually not used for regular teaching, so that the American quarter is, in the end, pretty much the same thing as a European trimester, or term.

It is often claimed that semesters are the normal pattern in many mainland European countries. In fact patterns vary quite a lot, not just between countries but also within them. Thus you can find examples of semesters and terms in most European countries. In some you even find 'Quad-rimesters', which, etymologically, should be periods of four months, and in fact are a more accurate description of what most of us describe as a semester.

So semesters are not a trendy American import, but a way of organising academic years which has been around a long time, on both sides of the Atlantic. They are in the news because, in recent years, their popularity has been growing rapidly in the UK, largely as a result of the move towards modular course structures.

How long are semesters? 34

While semesters ought to be six months long there is no universally accepted convention on the length of semesters. They can be as long or as short as you want them to be, though in the UK and the USA it is fairly generally accepted that academic years need to contain about thirty weeks if an appropriate amount of material is to be covered in sufficient depth.

Fifteen weeks is therefore the length of semesters in many semester-based systems.

This does not necessarily indicate fifteen weeks of teaching per semester. Particularly in universities which are modular most semester-based systems, and indeed term-based systems, allow time within the module for activities such as academic advice, induction, assessment, and so on. A fifteen week semester is therefore likely to contain twelve or thirteen weeks' teaching, sometimes with a Self-directed, or Private Study Week (the terminology varies) inserted to relieve what can otherwise be a long uninterrupted haul.

There are some systems which have semesters longer than fifteen weeks, but the difference between a fifteen and an eighteen week semester is likely to be more apparent than real. Anglia Polytechnic University's semesters contain teaching blocks of twelve or thirteen weeks, the remainder of the time being devoted to induction, assessment and associated meetings etc. In the end, the number of weeks is a less important consideration than such matters as the amount of learning to be undertaken, the time devoted to formal assessment, time available for counselling, etc.

When should the academic year start?   35

As with the length of semesters, there is no agreed 'right' answer to this question.

In the US, most semester-based universities start the first semester quite early, by British standards. Typically, it begins in early September and is completed before Christmas, so that the religious holiday can form the inter-semester break. A second semester can then comfortably be completed by late May, interrupted by a short Spring break, leaving the Summer free for students to concentrate on vacation, travel or earning; and academic staff on their research.

In much of mainland Europe, the year starts in October. The first semester is interrupted by a relatively short Christmas break, and ends in February, with the result that the inter-semester break fits neatly into the life-style of skiers among students and academic staff. It is worth pointing out, though, that fairly few universities in continental Europe operate modular systems. Their courses are typically conceived as year-long units. They therefore do not normally need the kind of break, with students out of the way and staff free to concentrate on marking, which is felt by most modular institutions to be essential.

In the UK the question of when the year should begin in semester-based systems has caused a degree of controversy.

Most of the universities which have operated semesters for some time superimpose semesters on the traditional October-to-June academic year. Many of them in fact operate only some of their courses on a semester basis, with the others sticking to the three-term year, and therefore have little choice over dates. Staffing arrangements, timetabling etc., would be impossibly complicated otherwise.

The advance of modularisation, however, has made more universities consider semesters. At the same time, pressure on universities to increase intakes without a commensurate growth in funds has focused attention on exploring ways of getting more students through the system without building more universities.

One result of these pressures was the establishment in 1993 of the Flowers Committee, whose task was to take a fundamental look at the shape of the academic year, and recommend a pattern more able to deliver the government's demands.

So what did Flowers recommend? 36

In the event, the Flowers Committee produced a less definitive report than many had hoped, and failed to give firm guidance on whether or not to semesterise, The report suggests that universities which did take that path should adopt as the 'ideal' pattern a first semester which could be completed before Christmas; a second semester of the same length; and a year pattern which could allow for a third semester as a means of using buildings more intensively.

Opinion among semesterising and modularising universities has tended to polarise around the 'broken back' model (a first semester beginning in October, punctuated by a two or three week Christmas break, and ending in late January/early February); and the 'early start' model in which a first semester completed before Christmas necessitates a shortening of the recruitment period for new students. Some institutions are moving to a 'staggered start' system, in which first year students begin the year later than those in later years.

'Broken Back'

Early October: Year starts
Ten weeks teaching to Christmas break

Christmas break three/four weeks

Five weeks teaching/assessment

Inter-semester break (one to three weeks)

Semester Two starts late February.

Three to six weeks teaching

Spring Break three to four weeks

Nine to twelve weeks teaching/assessment

Administration period

Year ends sometime in July.

'Early start'

Early September: Year starts
Fifteen weeks teaching/assessment

Christmas break/inter-semester break, four to six weeks for students, two to three for staff

Semester Two starts late January/early February

Approximately eight weeks teaching

Spring break one to four weeks

Approximately seven weeks teaching/assessment

Administration period

Year ends sometime in June

It is not clear at this point which pattern will win the day, though at the time of writing there were strong indications that most universities prefer an earlier start to the academic year, so that completion of a fifteen week semester before Christmas would be possible. Much will probably depend on developments over the release date for A level results, and/or major changes in the admissions process. In the meantime, controversy rages both between and within universities.

Few on either side of the great divide have much good to say about 'staggered start', including most of its supporters, who see it only as a necessary but short-lived evil, to enable early start to function in the period before the examining boards can manage to change.

So, for the UK there is as yet no easy answer to the question of when a semester-based year should start. It could be October, as now. It could be early September, if A level results can be brought forward. It could even be January, if the Admission system moves to a 'known results' basis. Watch this space!

How long should there be between semesters?   37

The question only really matters in the context of modular courses. If semesters are introduced in a non-modular context, then it is only a question of the rhythm of the academic year. For instance, European universities which run programmes which in most cases are designed to cover whole years, tend to give students a break at Christmas and in the Spring, even though both these holidays fall within semesters. The relative length of the two holidays and of the inter-semester break would appear not to matter too much. One could have long holidays and a short, or even no inter semester break, or do the reverse.

The case of modular universities is different. Most universities operating modular programmes would see the advantages of modularity as including regular feed-back to students. Add in the requirements of credit-accumulation systems, and you have powerful reasons why it is pretty well essential to be able to give students their assessment results for one semester before they start the following semester's programme. In systems where students choose, or can modify their programme each semester, the point is even stronger.

In modular contexts, therefore, the period required between semesters is whatever period it takes to complete the assessment process, notify students of the outcome, provide academic advice as appropriate and get the next semester's programme organised.

In a typical scheme involving 15-week semesters, Week 14 might be set aside for examinations. Many modules would probably be assessed in some way other than closed examination, but one would expect that all work to be marked would have been submitted by then. So, while students prepare themselves for the next semester, staff get down to marking. The time-scale of this operation depends on the scale of the scheme. In a large modular scheme, it might be something like this:

Assessment period.

Week One (Semester week 15) Internal marking

Week Two (First inter-semester week)
Consultation of external assessors.

Week Three (Second inter-semester week)
In-putting of moderated marks
Assessment Boards

Week 4 (Third inter-semester week)
Results communicated

Student counselling

That may look like quite a civilised time-scale. It is, provided everything goes smoothly but if it doesn't, and computers crash or records are lost or there is a postal strike it can be a race against time to get everything done.

There are, of course, ways of making the process simpler. For example, if you are operating a modular, credit accumulation system, there is no compelling reason why the external assessors' input should come at the end of a particular semester. If the essence of the external's role is to monitor the marking standards of the internal assessors, then in a system with multiple assessment points, this need not be done to a tight time-scale just before an Assessment Board or Final Awards Board, provided it is clear to students that marks fed back to them may be moderated later.

But whatever refinements are built into the process, the advice from modular institutions tends to be that it is not advisable to try to operate with fewer than three staff working weeks, and preferably four, between the completion of student assessments for one semester and the beginning of teaching for the next. We would strongly endorse this view, and urge a sceptical reaction to assurances from computer experts that anything else is feasible. To try to operate on a tighter time-scale is simply not worth it in terms of stress.

What is the 'third semester'? **38**

In a situation where governments are looking for low-cost ways of increasing the number of higher education students, the notion of using university premises more intensively is obviously attractive to them, if not to lecturers. So a number of ways of doing this have been investigated. In the UK, for example, the government is funding a number of experimental accelerated degree programmes which use a combination of techniques such as admitting students with advanced standing, using the summer period to provide a fourth term or third semester, accrediting previous academic and other experiences..

The Flowers Committee, which conducted perhaps the most thorough investigation of the implications of introducing a third semester so far, concluded that the introduction of a third semester might make sense, as a means of achieving an increased throughput of up to 50%, but also drew attention to the many and far reaching implications.

Unfortunately for the Flowers Committee, their report appeared just as the UK Government announced a slow-down to the expansion of university student numbers, thereby removing one of the principal justifications for the recommendation of the third semester.

So, there is little prospect that third semesters will become general in the UK for the foreseeable future. Nonetheless, they could come back on to the agenda in the UK or elsewhere at some point, so it is worthwhile looking at what Flowers had to say about them.

Flowers' starting point was that, given a fifteen week semester, then in theory three semesters can be fitted into a year. A third semester could allow a university to accommodate up to 50% more students, and allow the introduction of both accelerated two year degrees and decelerated one semester a year degrees. The norm would be for individual students to attend for two of the three semesters each year, with multiple entry points for new students.

So much could have been thought of by anyone. But Flowers followed through on many of the major implications of the expansion of universities' operating periods (see annex D, E and F). Among the factors considered are the increased cost involved in keeping libraries and student services fully operational through the summer, the need to think again about the scheduling of building maintenance work, since there would be no substantial period of reduced activity, the implications of keeping administrative teams operational, etc.

All of these factors raise major problems, which can only be solved at a reasonable economic cost if really substantial increases in student numbers are possible. Even then, the transitional costs involved in making the move are substantial, and it is clear from Flowers that in the early years of the change, average costs per student would be more likely to go up than down. But perhaps an even greater problem lies in the need for major changes to student attendance patterns. It does not take a lot of imagination to realise that if the norm is to be for students to attend two semesters per year, but universities to teach three, then the only way to operate economically (which implies a full student population all the time) is for student attendance patterns to vary. Flowers looks at the implications, and gives several examples of how things could be managed. Other patterns can be devised apart from the ones which feature in Flowers. But it is difficult to find any which do not necessitate the direction of students into different patterns of attendance. Some of these involve patterns which change according to the year of the course (Semesters one and two in Year One, two and three in Year Two, one and three in Year Three, for instance). Others involve dividing year groups so that not all attend simultaneously. All, obviously, put under threat some of the features which have characterised UK higher education until now, for example, progression through a course alongside fellow students, with senior or junior year-groups attending alongside, would be a thing of the past, producing a dramatically different student experience.

Won't the change from terms to semesters 39 be unmanageable?

Any change of this magnitude has the potential to be very disruptive. The extent to which it does in practice disrupt university life will depend on how successfully the difficulties have been foreseen and prepared for.

Of course, not all universities will face the same problems. Those which are not modularising will have a less complicated task in some ways, in that without the need to complete assessment processes at the end of each semester they will be able to introduce semesters within the old term patterns if they wish, allowing them to run terms and semesters side by side for a transitional period.

That said, however, it is difficult to see why any university which is not modularising its courses would see advantages in semesterisation sufficient to justify the potential disruption. So, semesterisation is likely to be taking place in the context of a move to modularity, and this complicates the process.

A common situation will be one where term-based courses with traditional final examinations are being replaced by modular courses or course-schemes with end-of-module assessment processes and credit accumulation. The complications in this move are that the two systems have different needs. Semester based modular courses need to avoid major interruptions at traditional holiday times (unless these can be made to coincide with the end of the semester), and to have a decent gap between semesters. Staff working in term-based systems like to have no interruption during term, and a decent gap between terms.

Given the above, it will immediately be clear that the two systems cannot easily run side by side. To run a semester based modular course with any real hope of success requires either an early start to the year, so that Christmas can provide the inter-semester break; or an inter-semester break probably in February. For term-based courses, a gap in February makes no sense, and an early start would make the Christmas break too long.

So the issue is how to manage the transition so as to cause as little disruption as possible to the lives of staff and students.

A number of compromise approaches suggest themselves, the most obvious being:

• During the transitional phase, why not run semesters within the term dates - i.e. Semester One would be the ten weeks of the first term, and five of the second. Since not all students would need assessing at the end of the semester (since some would still be on non-modular courses), it should be possible to run without an inter-semester gap for a while. Then we can move to a more sensible year structure when the old courses have been phased out.

• Start the first year of the new modular course three weeks earlier than the old term-based courses, so that the first semester can finish in Week Two of Term Two, be followed by a three-week break, and allow the second semester to finish simultaneously with the third term.

• Forget about the above. Let the two systems co-exist for a while, each following their own logic, until the term-based courses have run themselves out.

Each of these approaches creates problems.

The first sounds logical only to those who have no experience of assessment in a modular system. To anyone who has experienced the stress of marking a large number of scripts and then attending meetings and doing all the other things required between semesters, a three-week break looks short enough. The no-gap strategy, even when it is not taken literally (Week 15 may be called a counselling week, Week 1 an introductory week, to create a gap without appearing to) seems to us to be enormously risky and likely to put teaching staff under great stress.

The second also has several drawbacks. Starting early is problematical in itself unless a particular university is able to complete the admissions process untypically early. This might work, in the UK at least, for only a small number of very prestigious institutions. The rest have to depend, in various degrees, on the cumbersome and time-consuming 'Clearing' process. Until and unless both the Admissions system and the dates of A level examinations are changed, starting early will be very difficult. A further problem would be that of bringing students back after Christmas for two weeks of Semester One, followed by a three-week gap. This is not likely to be popular. Out of term time, students would either have to live away from home for the three weeks, without a grant, or they would have to go back home, which could involve considerable travel costs and accommodation difficulties. Such an arrangement could cause severe difficulties for the ever-increasing proportion of mature students.

The third compromise option avoids the problems of the other two, but raises plenty of its own, since it effectively lengthens the period during which staff will have teaching duties. It can only work if the semester year either starts before or finishes after the term-based year, or if vacations are varied between the two groups of students. Either way, staff end up teaching in more weeks and this will, in many cases, raise contractual problems. In many universities, including the former Polytechnics in the UK, staff can only be required to be in attendance for a fixed number of weeks per year. Both termly and semesterised years tend to use up all these weeks. If both run side by side, then either contractual time is over-run, or one needs to put staff into separate 'term' and 'semester' groups. Neither option seems either attractive or practicable.

The experience of Anglia Polytechnic University, which had a simpler task than many in that its courses were already modular on a termly basis, the best approach is the 'Big Bang', i.e. from a given point, all years of all courses change to a semester pattern, including the non-modular courses for which semesters are not necessarily logical.

This approach, of course, raises its own problems. But if students are given adequate forewarning, it will almost certainly be easier to solve these problems than those raised by the compromise positions outlined above.

Do semester dates need to be the same at all universities? 40

'No' is the short answer, any more than term dates ever were, though, certain things are made easier if dates are fairly similar throughout individual national systems of higher education. And, with the growing internationalisation of HE courses, it will increasingly be the case that international agreement on academic year structures will be desirable.

There are sevearal reason for this, the principal one being the expansion of modularity and credit accumulation and transfer in higher education.

Chapter 5

Policy questions

41   Why should we change from good old terms?

42   Why are so many universities changing over to semesters?

43   Don't holidays break up semesters unacceptably?

44   Aren't semesters only necessary if you modularise as well?

45   Where does credit transfer come in?

46   How can credit transfer operate between semester-based and term-based universities?

47   Don't semesters complicate overseas links?

Why should we change from good old terms?   41

There is absolutely no reason why any university, college or school should change unless it sees some educational value in doing so. Terms have worked for a long time, and there is no reason why they should not continue to do so.

Nonetheless it remains the case that increasing numbers of institutions in the UK and mainland Europe are moving over to semesters, and one of the driving forces behind this move in the UK is the spread of modularity.

In most modular systems assessment is completed within the module as are also the processes of student counselling. Given this, many academics feel that terms of ten weeks offer too short a period for all necessary processes to be properly completed, and that they tend to fragment the learning process to an undesirable degree.

In addition, terms, for technical reasons connected with the contractual conditions of lecturers in the UK's new universities, limit the time available between teaching periods. Lecturers need time to complete activities like assessment, curriculum development, course updating, etc. in the periods when students are not around. Experience in institutions running large modular schemes suggests that three weeks is the minimum desirable length of the turnaround period. Staff contracts which only allow for thirty-eight weeks of scheduled time per year mean that at some points in the three-term year things become very frantic indeed, and the slightest problem with, for example, the IT support for course administration can quickly become a disaster. The atmosphere of rush, and the nervous tension induced by it, can all too easily damage the learning experience for students.

Semesters offer some hope of improvement. If the year is divided into two rather than three, a long enough gap can be left between semesters. Staff can cope more equitably and rigorously with large numbers of scripts twice per year rather than three times, and slightly longer can be devoted to the process each time.

So the rush to semesterise is often linked to modularisation, though not always so. There are some modular institutions which remain committed to terms, often arguing that terms allow greater flexibility and a higher degree of student choice because they divide learning into small components. This is therefore a major philosophical difference from those who argue that ten week units fragment learning.

Modularity often encourages institutions to look towards semesterisation, but need not necessarily push them in that direction.

Non-modular institutions are under no particular pressure to semesterise, except insofar as they may want to keep study dates and patterns in line with those of most other institutions. In 1995, relatively few UK non-modular universities were proposing to semesterise, though it should be added that each time a survey is conducted, more universities are revealed to be planning to adopt modularity, so that we are talking about a reducing group. In mainland Europe, on the other hand, semesters are quite common despite the fact that very few institutions run modular courses.

Why are so many universities changing over to semesters?   **42**

In many, possibly most, cases the decision to introduce semesters follows or coincides with a decision to 'go modular'.

The reasons for this are twofold.

From the academic point of view it is often felt that in modular structures there is a danger of courses becoming too fragmented. The essence of a module is that it represents a self-contained learning experience, with assessment of the student taking place at the end of it, so that students receive feedback on their performance constantly throughout the course, and do not suffer the traumatic, make or break experience of traditional 'finals'.

However, if the modules are short, students get the feeling of being assessed nonstop, with no time for reflection or to digest what they have learned.

The other reason is a pragmatic one. In many instances, academic staff contracts require staff to teach for a maximum of thirty-six weeks per year, with a further two weeks available for administration. Given the need for a break of three weeks between teaching periods, it is easy to see that operating large modular schemes on a termly basis raises severe problems, especially when one adds in the need for administration weeks before teaching begins in October.

It is for these main reasons that universities, looking at the implications of modularity, have opted for semester-based delivery, so as to minimise the fragmentation of learning that occurs in some term-based systems, and a staff year which is divided on a pattern something like the following:

One week of Administration.

Fifteen weeks for Semester One.

Three working weeks inter-semester break.

Fifteen weeks Semester Two.

Three weeks administration
(Assessment Boards, etc.)

One week 'floating administration', to cover
admissions duties in the Summer vacation, etc.

Of course, not all universities have seen things this way. Some have opted for a shorter inter-semester break; some have introduced 'broken back' systems with no inter-semester break at all, in order to be able to run semesters alongside terms. But it is perhaps significant that the institutions most vocal about the need for a clear break between semesters, and for a period when staff can devote themselves to the necessary non-teaching duties without the distractions of teaching, are precisely those with experience of the complexity of operating large modular schemes.

Don't holidays break up semesters unacceptably? 43

It depends what you mean by 'unacceptably', since it is very difficult to find any semester pattern which can provide two uninterrupted periods of study. So semesters will always be broken up, and the only issue is how they are broken, and what is the effect of breaking them up.

In broad terms, the patterns currently being discussed in the UK fall predominantly into the two types described above, the so-called 'broken back', and the unbroken first semester. In both cases, the second semester is broken by the Spring holiday.

It is difficult to discuss rationally which of these approaches is better, since the timing of A level results means that adopting anything other than 'broken back' is very problematical anyway. However, there have been debates in a number of institutions which have focused on both academic and practical considerations. Some of the academic arguments advanced in favour of 'broken back' are:

- the Christmas vacation, coming after ten or eleven weeks, can provide time for reflection on and absorption of the material covered. It avoids the possibility that staff and students will become exhausted by a long period of uninterrupted teaching and learning, and more pragmatically, it preserves the traditional academic year, which fits well with the rest of the educational system.

- the second semester has to be broken anyway, so why such a fuss about the first one? It does not require any major change to the admissions process.

Among the arguments of supporters of the unbroken first semester are:

- far from being a time for reflection, the Christmas vacation is a time for eating, drinking and taking temporary work to make ends meet. It inevitably breaks up the academic year in a much more real sense than is true of the Spring vacation.

- if the conventional start date is preserved, the Christmas vacation comes very late in the teaching block. By the time students have settled back in, the twelve weeks of teaching are over. The weeks after Christmas are therefore likely to be wasted.

- exhaustion can be avoided by inserting a 'guided self-study week' at the midpoint of the semester.

- it is particularly important for first-year students not to have the first semester's teaching interrupted.

- the present admissions process is rapidly becoming unworkable under pressure from increased student numbers, so the question of meeting its needs is irrelevant.

Both sides are strongly committed to their views. Both sides quote the example of other countries where semesters have been established longer. Proponents of 'broken back' point to mainland Europe, where the first semester often ends in February. Supporters of the unbroken system point out that few European universities operate modular systems. American universities, whose systems are much more like UK modular degrees, have largely moved away from broken back, in favour of a first semester completed before Christmas.

Not surprisingly, a number of universities have adopted compromise positions. Some, notably the University of Surrey and some of its associated institutions, are going for a staggered start. Others, such as Anglia Polytechnic University, have found ways of fitting in twelve teaching weeks for all years before Christmas. But these compromise positions raise their own problems. The staggered start makes induction of new students a very complicated process; staff are busy at the crucial time; rooms are in use; students of later years are not as easily available to help. And fitting in twelve teaching weeks before Christmas means either that the Autumn term modules have to rely entirely on continuous assessment, or that the exams are held immediately after the Christmas break, which is not popular with students.

It is because of these factors that these compromise positions are seen, even by their advocates, as short-term solutions to a problem which needs to be resolved through a much more radical approach. It is likely that universities will continue to press for changes to the timing of A level exams (the vocational qualifications raise fewer problems) and to the admissions process such that an unbroken first semester becomes possible.

Aren't semesters only necessary if you   **44** modularise as well?

Semesters are not necessary to modularisation, though many would feel they help the‑process, by making it possible to run larger modules than are possible in a termly system.

They are simply an alternative way of organising the year.   They suit modularity, but can be operated successfully in non-modular circumstances, as is shown by the number of European universities which have run on semesters for a long time, in many cases without ever thinking seriously about going modular.

More serious arguments in their favour consider, for example, their potential for reducing the amount of vacation time during the year and thus leading to an earlier finish to teaching and a longer unbroken period in the summer for scholarly activity - though it has to be said that this benefit is largely illusory, due to the inexplicable attachment of some people to the idea of having a decent break at Christmas, or going away at Easter.

Another attraction for some is the possibility of allowing accelerated progression for some students, or flexible study patterns for all, by introducing a third semester. More on this later. For the moment let's just note that a degree course lasting six semesters can, theoretically, be compressed into two years each containing three semesters.   A nine-term course cannot be compressed as easily - at least, not without some pretty ingenious arrangements. Fitting in three semesters is much less simple than it sounds. Nonetheless, it is a serious argument in favour of semesters for some people.

Semesters are never necessary, in an absolute sense, but in some circumstances have advantages over terms. As a framework for modularity, they can reduce some of the pressure of tight assessment schedules (you only assess twice a year, rather than three times with terms).   They also can be used in ways which fragment study of a discipline less than termly modules tend to do. But in the end, what matters is how well the scheme has been designed overall, and how much thought has gone into the design of individual modules. A badly designed module, overloaded with content and assessed in a cumbersome way, will turn students off whether it lasts for a term, a semester or a year. Conversely, the success of the modular scheme at Oxford Brookes shows that a termly system, operated by experienced staff with good IT support, can function smoothly, with a high degree of student satisfaction.

So, you pay your money and you make your choice. Our vote goes for semesters, but not by a massive margin. You may feel differently.

Where does credit transfer come in? 45

Credit transfer is the process whereby a university gives credit for work done in another institution, in a systematic way (in that it goes beyond the old notion of admission with advanced standing).

Credit transfer has long been a feature of the USA higher education, though there the norm is for each university to have its own system for assessing credit. Credits earned at one university are frequently, but not necessarily or automatically, accepted by another.

In the UK, credit accumulation tends to arrive with modularity. Credit transfer usually comes with it. There is no absolutely essential link between credit accumulation systems and modularity nor, in the last analysis, between either of these and credit transfer. So long as credit can be measured in some acceptable way, it can be transferred. But credit transfer is obviously easier if all universities within a particular system are operating according to certain basic agreed norms, such as the value of credits. If they also operate, as in the UK, a system of external assessors designed to ensure that standards at the various universities are broadly in line with each other, then credit transfer is further facilitated, and it becomes possible to think in terms of national credit transfer schemes.

The need for such schemes arises from the changes higher education is undergoing, which are more dramatic in some parts of the world than in others, largely because of the different starting points. In the UK they are felt particularly keenly as the higher education system moves away from being a small, relatively well-resourced system catering for a minority group of well-qualified students supported by the State, studying full-time for three years, and becomes instead an underfunded, broad based system, catering for the mass participation of a student body no longer fully supported by the State and including many more part-time students. Add to this a growing feeling among employers that their needs are no longer adequately met by students who graduate at the age of 21 or 22, never to study again, and you have a set of powerful reasons for thinking that the study patterns of the future are likely to include much more part-time study, much more working one's way through university, much more dropping in and out of higher education as circumstances change, much more topping up of skills during a working career, etc.

In these circumstances, credit transfer is likely to become increasingly important, since it is likely that many of higher education's future clients will move around the country, or even the world, in the course of their studies. The traditional pattern of academic years may also change. In a system based on modularity and large numbers of part-time students it is necessary, and perfectly feasible, to allow study to start at the beginning of any semester.

If this vision of the future is anywhere near accurate, then clearly higher education systems will need to adapt to provide the flexibility needed. Transfer between institutions would be much easier if all operated on the basis of fifteen week semesters, all kept to more or less the same dates, and all operated modular, credit accumulation systems with agreed credit tariffs.

So the introduction of semesters certainly does not require any harmonisation of dates. But developments in higher education would seem to make harmonisation a good idea, if it is to genuinely serve the needs of its client group.

How can credit transfer operate between   46
semester- and term-based universities?

The problem of operating credit transfer between varying systems is easy to exaggerate. Given a will to make it work, credit transfer need not be a complicated process.

The key to the whole thing is that there should be an agreed accounting method. If all universities use the same one, life becomes easier. But even where this is absent the problems are soluble, and not made much more difficult by a mismatch between terms and semesters.

All universities have a notion of what constitutes a normal year's programme for a full-time student. It is therefore perfectly possible to calculate what proportion of a course has been completed and to assign a value to it, which can then be translated into a different currency to suit either terms or semesters.

The complications which arise concern the length of the course rather than the calculation of credit. Transfer from a term-based university to a semester system can create problems of timing whose severity will depend on the term or semester dates of particular institutions. But the worst problem that could arise for a full-time student would occur if the student moved from a term to a semester system after one term of an academic year. He/she might then have completed one third of a year's work in University A, and only be able to enrol for half a year's programme at University B. This problem could readily be solved by some combination of extending the course and accelerating the study.

So our answer is that it should not be particularly difficult, and certainly much less complicated than some of the things the more progressive universities have been into for some time now, such as the accreditation of both workplace learning, and prior learning (APL).

Don't semesters complicate overseas links? 47

What really complicates overseas links is the mismatch between national systems, which exists whether particular institutions use terms or semesters.

Student and staff exchanges between universities in different countries are therefore more complicated than they would be if dates and systems were harmonised.

The difficulties caused by the mismatch of systems can be got round with a bit of ingenuity. But there is no doubt that a lot of unnecessary effort has to be put into balancing the programmes of students who might, in a given year, do a programme which takes them to more than one country. They may easily end up able to complete one semester in one country, and a term in another. They might also end up doing two terms and one semester.

The semesterisation of UK universities would make life simpler for those planning exchanges but only if similar patterns operated in all countries using semesters.

The most common pattern in continental Europe is for Semester One to start in October, and to finish in February. Semester Two then starts late February.

In the USA, it is more common for Semester One to begin earlier, and to be completed before Christmas, with Semester Two beginning in January.

In the UK, terms remain for the moment the most common pattern. Semesters are rapidly catching up, with no clear indication as yet whether in the long term 'broken back' will prevail, or a pattern more like the American one.   A factor in the decision could be the desirability of exchanging with continental Europe, which might argue for broken back; or with the US, which would argue for a semester completed before

Christmas. An institution with links, or hoping to develop links, in both continents would have problems.

In an ideal world, agreement would be reached on a common pattern to operate throughout Europe and the US at least, and ideally throughout the world though matching the requirements of the two hemispheres would be complex. To enable UK universities to link with most European and US institutions,the first semester would need to be completed before Christmas, and the second one to begin in late February. This would give British universities a long Christmas vacation, but would make exchanges workable in any direction for British and American students. Continental Europeans could slot into either British semester at the expense, possibly, of losing their February break. If they wanted to go to the USA, a first semester exchange would be possible, but not a second as the US second semester starts before continental Europeans have finished their first.

But though this system could work, it could not be implemented easily. As we have indicated elsewhere, for UK universities, completing a fifteen-week semester before Christmas is only possible if there are major changes to the timetable for release of A level results. And the long Christmas vacation would definitely rule out any possibility of a third semester, as well as putting in a long gap which might be unacceptable to part-time students and their employers.

In summary, semesters do not seem to make exchanges more difficult. They can be made to make them easier, but only if the UK adopts a particular pattern which would require changes to the A level system, and a longer inter-semester break than many consider desirable.

Chapter 6

Staff and student questions

48　Can anyone tell us what advantages semesterisation can possibly offer to students?

49　Won't semesterisation make the student admissions process unmanageable?

50　So what kind of student admissions system could we move to?

51　Wouldn't semesterisation increase the time students have to live on their already inadequate grants?

52　Wouldn't the introduction of the third semester increase staff workloads?

53　What is this awful notion of the 'staggered start'?

Can anyone tell us what advantages semesterisation can possibly offer for students?   48

It is difficult to see advantages or, indeed, particular disadvantages in semesterising non-modular courses. Proponents of semesterisation tend, on the whole, to also be fans of modularity. Their answers to this question therefore usually presuppose that it is being asked in a modular context. They usually focus on the following features:

i   One of the virtues of modularity is that it puts students more in control of their courses, through the facility offered by most modular schemes for students to have choice over the modules taken. Schemes vary in the points at which they let students choose. Some for example get them to choose the whole programme for years 2 and 3 during the first year. But even these usually let students modify their programme at the start of each term or semester. Choice can be disastrous if it is not informed by clear advice from staff. This can be more easily provided if there are fewer choice points. In a semester-based system, a three-year course will involve six choice points. A term-based system will have nine.

ii   Semester-length modules enable topics to be studied in more depth, and allow more time for reflection, than is possible in a termly system.

iii Students on modular programmes sometimes complain about being over-assessed. Even when the amount of assessment is no greater, in total, than would be normal for a non-modular course, its frequency can lead to a situation in which students become obsessed with assessment and lose sight of the fact that they are supposed to be receiving an education as well as accumulating credit. Semesterisation can help reduce this tendency, by focusing on module results twice per year rather than three times.

iv Semesterisation can (but does not necessarily) facilitate an earlier end to the academic year, thus freeing students to undertake seasonal employment at an earlier point, as well as potentially offering a longer period of unbroken employment or for reflection and consolidation of learning.

v   Some students, particularly the increasing number of mature students entering HE in mid-career, or between careers, often with accredited prior learning (APL), see no particular virtue in studying for three years rather than two. If they are able to study at an accelerated pace, there seems no particular reason to prevent them doing so. If a 'third semester' is offered, they have a neat framework within which to accelerate their course - neater, from most points of view, than can be offered by a 'fourth term'

Won't semesterisation make the student admissions process unmanageable? 49

Clearly there is nothing about semesterisation which, in itself, makes the admissions process unmanageable. If there were, universities which operate semesters, in the UK and elsewhere, would have collapsed long ago.

The question nonetheless is worth asking in a UK context, if it is taken to mean semesterisation on the 'ideal' lines favoured by Flowers.

As we have seen, this model would indeed make the present admissions system pretty well unmanageable. This is why it has not been adopted and why some institutions have moved to a staggered start as an interim position.

What happens in the longer term depends upon whether the universities' desire for an unbroken first semester wins out over the reluctance of the A level Boards to change the timing of their examinations. A big factor in fuelling this reluctance is the spread of the modular approach to A levels and the consequent increase in the amount of continuous assessment in A level courses, which is one of the reasons for pressure within schools to complete A level courses later than at present - an outcome which would exacerbate the difficulties.

Another factor in the situation is the widespread dissatisfaction with the Clearing system, which means that for many students the culmination of a long process of study and careful consideration of particular universities and what they have to offer is an undignified scramble for a place at whatever university is willing to take them, with no time to learn anything much about it before turning up to Day One of the course.

So what kind of student admissions system could we move to?   **50**

There are approaches which could potentially resolve the admissions problem. Leaving aside the really radical ideas, such as open access to university for all qualified candidates, there are, alternative systems which could bridge the gap between the desires of universities, schools and A level Boards. Both are being considered and investigated by the Universities and Colleges Admissions Service. They are:

i   An approach similar to that used in Ireland, designed to adjust the untidy Clearing system. The basic approach would be that universities would decide in advance how many students they would take, with what grades. Students would choose a number of universities they might wish to attend, in order of preference. Once results were known, a computer would match students to the highest preference university for which they had qualified.

     This approach has some obvious advantages over Clearing. Students would not have to make last minute decisions on offers from universities they had never previously thought about, as happens all too often in Clearing. Universities, unless they pitched their demands ridiculously high, would be much more likely to achieve intake targets so long as they made reasonable entrance requirements.

     On the other hand, it would depend on the reliability of a very rapid and efficient computer sort.

ii   The other approach considered by UCAS is a system based on known results. This would involve students applying for HE places only after A level results are known, which would remove all need for conditional offers.

155

The attractions of this from every point of view are obvious. Its major drawback is that it could not conceivably be operated on anything like the present time-scale. Assuming courses in schools continue to end in the summer, and exam results to appear in late August, the only way this system could operate would be on the basis of HE courses beginning later. The implications of this are so far-reaching as to almost certainly make this a nonstarter for the foreseeable future. For example, a later start, if applied to all years, would make an unbroken first semester impossible, and we have seen that an unbroken first semester is something most universities want. An alternative might be for only first-year students to begin later - but then all the objections to staggered start (see below) would apply, with a vengeance. A third option would be to begin the academic year in January - but how viable would it be either to have a long summer vacation in the middle of each year of study or to shorten the summer vacation and have a long vacation in November/December? Yet another option would be to start the first year in January, and shorten courses to two and a half years - but this would require a wholesale reassessment of what is meant by the concept of degree-level study.

All in all, it seems unlikely that this option will find favour.

So, although semesterisation itself is pretty neutral in terms of its impact on admissions systems, there are reasons for believing that the UK system of admissions will have to change, though in quite what direction is by no means clear at this stage.

Wouldn't semesterisation increase the   51
time students have to live on their already
inadequate grants?

It should not.

In most term-based systems, the academic year covers thirty weeks. Year-end exams sometimes lop a bit off the end of this, but in term-based modular schemes it is not uncommon for assessments to take place in Week 10, compelling students to stick it out to the bitter end. Some even have assessments in Week 11.

Semesters of fifteen weeks thus need not bring any change to the length of time students have to be in attendance. This is even true of Anglia Polytechnic University, which is going for eighteen-week semesters, but as replacement for twelve-week terms.

In any case, the biggest single expense for most students these days is rent, and it seems to be the case that not only most private landlords/ladies, but also many university halls of residence operate on forty-week tenancies, a fact which makes the question largely redundant anyway. A better question might be that of how much longer anyone will be able to afford to live away from home as a student.

Wouldn't the introduction of a third   **52**
semester increase staff workloads?

The great fear of many HE lecturers is that an extended academic year would require them to teach for longer.

This fear is based in the suspicion that they would eventually be required to teach in all three semesters.

One can only speculate on the degree to which such fears may prove to be justified. If the view that teaching and research are linked activities, with mutually beneficial spin-offs, remains current, then it would clearly have to be the case that lecturing staff would each work in only two of the three semesters, devoting the third to research and scholarly activity. This would imply that academic staff numbers would rise alongside student numbers, though given the financial squeeze on most universities throughout the world, at a slower rate.

However, such a model only works if government funds the expanded HE work-force not only for teaching, but also for research activity. How likely is this, in the current financial climate? Not very, one might think, raising the possibility of the appointment of specialist staff either to teach, or to undertake research, with only a minority doing both. Were this to come about, the possibility of some staff being required to teach throughout an extended year might become more real.

We think this is unlikely for the foreseeable future, given the degree of resistance to such a change likely among HE staff. There are already real problems in securing sufficient funding for research. Workloads will undoubtedly get heavier as student numbers rise as a result of underfunding, but in the medium term we do not expect to see the appointment of staff to pure teaching posts covering more than thirty weeks in the year.

Whether we are right in this or not, the introduction of a third semester would clearly change the lives of academics fairly drastically. Just as students would have to get used to the loss of cohort identity, so would lecturers have to get used to not having all their colleagues around simultaneously. Given that a principal argument in favour of the third semester is the more intensive use of accommodation, the sharing of staff offices would become the norm. What would be one person's office in two semesters would be someone else's in the third. The logistics of this would be so complicated that it might even be the case that very few people would have a permanent base, changing office every year or even every semester. Most people think this will have a negative effect on the notion of academic community.

So, though we do not feel that a third semester would be likely in itself to increase teaching loads for individual lecturers, it is clear that it would affect their professional lives in a whole host of other ways, and profoundly change the nature of the HE experience both for them and for their students.

What is this awful notion of the 'staggered start'?   53

The 'staggered start' is an idea peculiar to the UK. It arose from the conflicting requirements of semesterisation and the UK Admissions process.

In the UK the present admissions system is complex. Conditional offers are made to students on the basis of predicted A level results. When results are published in mid-August those who have not achieved the grades required by their chosen university have to seek admission via the Clearing system, in which students search frantically for an institution willing to take them, and universities seek desperately for students in some subjects while secretly hoping that others will disappear from those which have over-recruited.

This process takes time, with the result that most UK universities would find it difficult to begin their academic year much before late September, and some are still recruiting at the beginning of October.

When considering semesterisation, most universities agree with the Flowers Committee, that ideally the first fifteen-week semester should be concluded before Christmas. Unfortunately the admissions system makes this very difficult to achieve for first-year students. But of course the problems caused by the admissions system are largely confined to first-year students, which led a number of universities to look for ways of starting the first semester early for students in later years, with a delayed start for the new first-year students.

There are a number of ways in which this can be achieved, all of them more or less problematical. One option is to run a shorter first semester for the first years, offering introductory modules which may not be assessed. Modular purists object to this approach on the grounds that making that semester's modules different from others makes it more difficult than it ought to be for students to begin a programme at any other point than the beginning of Semester One. Others have proposed bringing first-year students back for assessment immediately after Christmas, in a period which would be vacation for the later years, so that all years could start the second semester together. The problems of this approach concern mainly the inter-semester break, and the drawn-out assessment period it implies from the staff point of view. Still others have offered refinements of this approach, including suggestions of a first year of two fourteen week semesters.

The fact that universities are willing to even contemplate some of these suggestions is a strong indication of their overwhelming preference for an unbroken first semester. The fact that most have, in the end, rejected the staggered start is evidence of the great difficulties they see in it. These range from the obvious academic drawbacks to some highly practical considerations involving such factors as tenancy agreements for student accommodation; the difficulty of offering an induction programme when staff are already teaching and students of later years learning, and many large teaching rooms are being used already.

Very few have not been deterred by these difficulties. Among those who have taken their courage in both hands and staggered the start is the University of Surrey, along with some of its associated institutions. At the time of writing, it remains to be seen how successful this arrangement will be, but what seems clear is that the authorities at Surrey, like others who have adopted or considered adopting a staggered start, see it very much as an interim measure, and certainly not as a permanent solution. Their hope is that the schools' examination system will change fairly quickly so as to make an earlier start to the academic year possible. While waiting for this to happen, they are willing to pay the price of the staggered start.

References

Becher, T
& Kogan, M
Process and Structure in Higher Education Routledge
1992

Bluck, R et al
'Information Skills in Academic Libraries: A teaching and
learning role in higher education'
SEDA Paper 82 Staff and Education Development Association May 1994 Birmingham

Davidson, G
'Credit Accumulation and Transfer and the Student Experience" in Barnett, R (Ed) 1992 *Learning to Effect* SRHE &
Open University Press

ESRC
*Research Specification for the ESRC Learning Society :
Knowledge and Skills for Employment Programme"* Economic & Social Research Council 6 May 1994

Flowers, Lord
The Review of the Academic Year
HEFCE, November 1993

Gibbs, G
Teaching more students project
PCFC, London & OCSD 1991

Gibbs, G
Improving the Quality of Student Learning
Technical and Education Services Ltd. Bristol 1992

Gillies, C
'A Module for Action' in *Teaching News*, EMU, Oxford
Brookes University No.35 Autumn 1993

Laurillard, D
Rethinking University Teaching
Routledge 1993

O'Neil, M &
Pennington, G
*Evaluating Teaching and Courses from an Active
Learning Perspective* CVCP, USDTU 1992

Parlett, M   'Evaluation as Illumination' in Tawney, D (Ed)
Hamilton, D   *Curriculum Evaluation To-day: Trends and Implications*
Macmillan   1974

Ramsden, Paul   *Learning to Teach in Higher Education*
Routledge 1992

Robbins, Lord   *Higher Education : Report of the Committee on Higher Education*   HMSO, London 1963

Theodossin, E   *The Modular Market*
FESC, Coombe Lodge, Bristol 1986

THES   *Report on the Labour Party paper 'Opening Doors to a Learning Society'* T H E S, 29 July 1994

Trow, Martin   American Higher Education - past, present and future
Studies in Higher Education Vol.14, No.1, 1989

Wingspread   *An American Imperative : Higher Expectations for Higher Education*   The Johnson Foundation, USA 1993

Winter, Richard   'The problem of educational levels (Part 2) : A New Framework for Credit Accumulation in Higher Education' *Journal of Further and Higher Education* 18(1) Spring 1994

Wordsworth, Y   *Everyday Evaluation on the Run*
Action Research Issues Association Inc., Melbourne, Australia (1991)

Yorke, Mantz   'Quality in Higher Education : A Conceptualisation and Some Observations on the Implementation of a Sectoral Quality System'
Journal of Further and Higher Education 16 (2), Summer 1992